"Exuding biblical truth, theological insight, and historical understanding, Joyce Ann Zimmerman guides us through the rich mystery of the gathered body of Christ. This book is the product of a seasoned writer and worshiper who knows how to be accessible without being simplistic."

— C. MICHAEL HAWN
Perkins School of Theology

"Transdenominational, practical, and irenic. . . . Zimmerman offers a clear portrait of the complexity of worship in the current North American context and opens a path to reenvision worship that is rooted in baptism, inspired by Scripture, and full of gladness. Useful for worship leaders, worship committees, and students of all kinds."

— MARTHA MOORE-KEISH
Columbia Theological Seminary

"Unapologetically Catholic and unabashedly ecumenical. . . . Through biblically based, historically informed, and theologically rooted insights and wisdom, Zimmerman clearly defines worship and its constitutive elements. . . . A must-read for clergy, laity, worship leaders, church musicians, and any serious student of worship!"

— JAMES ABBINGTON
Candler School of Theology

The CALVIN INSTITUTE OF CHRISTIAN WORSHIP LITURGICAL STUDIES Series, edited by John D. Witvliet, is designed to promote reflection on the history, theology, and practice of Christian worship and to stimulate worship renewal in Christian congregations. Contributions include writings by pastoral worship leaders from a wide range of communities and scholars from a wide range of disciplines. The ultimate goal of these contributions is to nurture worship practices that are spiritually vital and theologically rooted.

PUBLISHED

The Pastor as Minor Poet: Texts and Subtexts in the Ministerial Life
  M. Craig Barnes

Arts Ministry: Nurturing the Creative Life of God's People
  Michael J. Bauer

Touching the Altar: The Old Testament and Christian Worship
  Carol M. Bechtel, Editor

Resonant Witness: Conversations between Music and Theology
  Jeremy S. Begbie and Steven R. Guthrie, Editors

God against Religion: Rethinking Christian Theology through Worship
  Matthew Myer Boulton

From Memory to Imagination: Reforming the Church's Music
  C. Randall Bradley

By the Vision of Another World: Worship in American History
  James D. Bratt, Editor

Inclusive yet Discerning: Navigating Worship Artfully
  Frank Burch Brown

What Language Shall I Borrow? The Bible and Christian Worship
  Ronald P. Byars

A Primer on Christian Worship: Where We've Been, Where We Are,
Where We Can Go
  William A. Dyrness

Christian Worship Worldwide: Expanding Horizons, Deepening Practices
  Charles E. Farhadian, Editor

Gather into One: Praying and Singing Globally
  C. Michael Hawn

The Touch of the Sacred: The Practice, Theology, and Tradition
of Christian Worship
  F. Gerrit Immink

The Substance of Things Seen: Art, Faith, and the Christian Community
  Robin M. Jensen

Our Worship
  Abraham Kuyper, Edited by Harry Boonstra

Wonderful Words of Life: Hymns in American Protestant History and Theology
  Richard J. Mouw and Mark A. Noll, Editors

Discerning the Spirits: A Guide to Thinking about Christian Worship Today
  Cornelius Plantinga Jr. and Sue A. Rozeboom

Evangelical versus Liturgical? Defying a Dichotomy
  Melanie C. Ross

Voicing God's Psalms
  Calvin Seerveld

My Only Comfort: Death, Deliverance, and Discipleship in the Music of Bach
  Calvin R. Stapert

A New Song for an Old World: Musical Thought in the Early Church
  Calvin R. Stapert

An Architecture of Immanence: Architecture for Worship and Ministry Today
  Mark A. Torgerson

A More Profound Alleluia: Theology and Worship in Harmony
  Leanne Van Dyk, Editor

Christian Worship in Reformed Churches Past and Present
  Lukas Vischer, Editor

We Have Seen His Glory: A Vision of Kingdom Worship
  Ben Witherington III

The Biblical Psalms in Christian Worship:
A Brief Introduction and Guide to Resources
  John D. Witvliet

Worship with Gladness: Understanding Worship from the Heart
  Joyce Ann Zimmerman

Worship with Gladness

Understanding Worship from the Heart

Joyce Ann Zimmerman

William B. Eerdmans Publishing Company
Grand Rapids, Michigan / Cambridge, U.K.

Published 2014 by
WM. B. EERDMANS PUBLISHING CO.
2140 Oak Industrial Drive N.E., Grand Rapids, Michigan 49505 /
P.O. Box 163, Cambridge CB3 9PU U.K.
www.eerdmans.com

Printed in the United States of America

19 18 17 16 15 14   7 6 5 4 3 2 1

Library of Congress Cataloging-in-Publication Data

Zimmerman, Joyce Ann, 1945-
Worship with gladness: understanding worship from the heart /
Joyce Ann Zimmerman.
pages   cm.
— (The Calvin Institute of Christian Worship liturgical studies series)
Includes bibliographical references and index.
ISBN 978-0-8028-6984-5 (pbk.: alk. paper)
1. Worship.   I. Title.
BV10.3.Z56   2014
248.3 — dc23
2014016341

Contents

Foreword by John D. Witvliet   xiii

Introduction   1

1. Worship: Withering or Greening?   11

THE ISSUE: WHAT, REALLY, IS WORSHIP?   11

A CLARIFICATION: WORSHIP AND/OR LITURGY?   19

THE DATA: WHAT DO WE SAY ABOUT WORSHIP?   31

WORSHIP NEEDS: ARE THERE ELEMENTS
WE SOMETIMES FORGET?   36

     Prayer   37

     Profession   40

     Confession   42

     Intercessions   44

     Blessings   45

     Mission   47

     Silence   47

SO WHAT, REALLY, IS WORSHIP?   50

2. God's Word: A Primer on Worship?   53

THE ANCIENT CODE: WORSHIP DRAWS US
INTO GOD'S HOLINESS, GOD'S VERY LIFE   58

The Psalm-Songs: Ancient Prayers Teach Us
About Worship   65

  Ascendency Psalms: Elements of Worship   65

  Psalms of Lament: A Structure of Worship   70

  Thanksgiving Psalms: For What Do We Give Thanks?   73

John 4:24: From Human Encounter
to Jesus as Messiah-Savior   76

Heavenly Worship: Multitudes Forever Sing
God's Praises   79

3. **Who We Are before God:
"Do You Not Know . . . ?"**   83

  Our Common Baptismal Identity   84

  The Saving Mystery of Christ   90

  A New and Shared Vision of Worship   96

    Paschal Mystery in the Constitution
    on the Sacred Liturgy   101

    Liturgy in the Rhythm of the Whole Christian Life 102

    The Celebration of the Whole Body   103

    Full, Conscious, and Active Participation   104
      "Active" Participation   106
      "Conscious" Participation   108
      "Full" Participation   109

4. **Being Together before God: Is Worship
Making a Difference in How We Live?**   115

  Worship Bursting out the Doors   117

The First Challenge: Increased Understanding
and Living of the Saving Mystery of Christ 118

The Second Challenge: Celebrating Worship Well 122

The Third Challenge: Engaging Worship Education 123

The Fourth Challenge: Worship Bursting Its Doors 125

WORSHIP IN ACTION 129

WORSHIP AND DOING JUSTICE 133

First, a (Long) Note on Justice 133

New Selves Living Justly 138

WORSHIP AND MISSION 139

Some Key Vocabulary 140

Kingdom/Reign of God 140

Eschatology 141

Salvation 142

Mission 143

Evangelization 144

Worship and Life and Mission 144

Conclusion 149

DESCRIBING CHRISTIAN WORSHIP 150

THE CHALLENGES THAT A FULLER
UNDERSTANDING OF THE
NATURE OF WORSHIP BRING 153

Index of Subjects 156

Index of Biblical References 159

Foreword

Reflecting on Worship's Meaning and Purpose

As Joyce Ann Zimmerman observes, starting a conversation about worship's deep meaning and purpose is no easy assignment. It is relatively easy for churchgoers to talk about things like the style of worship or their musical or artistic preferences or their opinions about their own leaders or presiders in worship. But trying to steer the conversation deeper — toward recognition of the core elements in worship or the ways in which we both address and are addressed by God in worship — is often extremely challenging.

Part of this difficulty is understandable. Christian worship transcends description. It is full of wonder that can't be captured adequately in words. It is good not to speak too quickly or glibly about its deeper purposes and dynamics.

But part of this difficulty also arises because many Christian communities are not convinced that reflecting on the deeper dynamics of worship is all that valuable. When we don't practice how to have those conversations, we lack the motivation and capacity to do so.

Here are a few reasons why this avoidance is misguided, and why theological reflection on worship's deep purpose and dynamics can be so fruitful.

1. *Reflecting on a practice shapes how we perceive the practice, what we pay attention to.* During baseball games, I may become mesmerized by the type font used on the scoreboard or the color of the package of the peanuts. But few would argue that this is the

ideal center of my attention at a baseball game. While these may be benign interests, baseball aficionados would much rather have me pay attention to the beauty of a well-thrown curve ball, the effective execution of bunt, and a hundred other nuances of the game. Likewise in worship, whatever else we may be attending to, we miss a great deal if we do not learn to notice how God not only receives but also prompts and perfects our worship, or how worship functions to strengthen a marriage-like covenantal relationship between God and the gathered community.

2. *Reflecting on a practice amplifies the potential of that practice to shape and form us.* All practices form us, but not all practices form us equally. If I go to a gym, I may well stumble upon a great workout plan and be formed into a fine athlete. But if I learn how exercises form me, I can be a much better steward of that formative physical activity. Similarly, worship shapes us, whether or not we reflect on it. But reflecting on it can help us notice, testify about, and lean into the ways that participation can sanctify us.

3. *Reflection on a practice strengthens our capacity to deepen the practice.* Few people really like rote teaching. We are blessed by teachers who reflect on their pedagogy, and pay attention not just to how teachers teach, but to how learners learn. Likewise, few people really cherish communal worship practices that are legalistic on the one hand or sloppy and sentimental on the other. We are blessed by congregational leaders who reflect on worship and pay attention to the ways in which it can embody deep biblical wisdom, in ways that avoid fussiness and sloppiness.

4. *Reflection on a practice helps us root out false and destructive forms of*

practice. Sub-par dieticians have led people who want to lose weight into all sorts of pernicious, self-destructive habits. It takes considerable medical expertise to discern which kinds of diets can really build a sustainable, healthy way of life. Similarly, sub-par worship leaders have led people into all sorts of spiritually self-destructive habits, reinforcing racism, narcissism, intolerance, hypocrisy, superstition, and a thousand other awful "isms." Praise God for faithful believers over the centuries who have reflected deeply on worship and found ways to resist this, promoting forms of worship that foster hospitality, wonder, mutual love, and self-giving.

5. *Reflecting on the practice of Christian worship in particular helps us discover (again and again) the gifts we've been given.* We recognize the sheer depths of God's love for us in Jesus, the sheer beauty of God's self-giving embrace, the sheer wonder of the way the Holy Spirit works to help us resist the temptation not to curve in on ourselves. Just as reflection on baseball or cooking or music or art can help us savor what we experience, so too reflection on worship can help us perceive more deeply the stunning grace that we celebrate in worship.

Theological reflection on corporate worship practices can take many forms, many of them informal and woven into the fabric of daily life: paragraph-long teaching notes in church or parish bulletins, four-minute lessons to young children or new Christians about an aspect of worship, short teaching moments in choir or worship team rehearsals — and many more!

There is also great value in deeper reflection that can feed, nourish, and strengthen those informal moments of reflection. And that is where this book comes in. Perhaps you are a new Christian wondering what worship is all about; perhaps you are a leader who shapes these informal moments of learning all the time; perhaps you are a veteran Christian who wants to grow beyond "auto-pilot" worship on Sunday; or perhaps you are looking for a book for study group or spiritual retreat. In each of these cases, this book offers an invitation to enter into the kinds of conversations that promise to renew and strengthen your own full, conscious, and active participation in worship. May God's Spirit use your engagement with this book not only to strengthen your faith, but also to enrich the community in which you live and worship.

A Catholic Voice in the Ecumenical or Trans-Denominational Choir

One final note: this book arose out of and is designed to contribute to a very trans-denominational conversation about worship. How grateful we can be that in addition to conversations within our own traditions and denominations (which are essential), we also have the opportunity to learn together across denominational lines. I am grateful for Joyce's contribution as a Catholic theologian, just as I am blessed by Joyce's reading of my work as a Protestant theologian.

To be sure, Catholic, Reformed, Methodist, Baptist, Presbyterian, Pentecostal, Anglican, and Mennonite Christians (and many others) have significant theological differences, and it is important not to simply dismiss these as unimportant. Both Joyce and I would warmly encourage each reader of this book to engage deeply with sources from his/her own tradition (perhaps alongside of reading this book).

It is also true that Christians across the spectrum of denominations share many convictions and practices. We worship Jesus as Lord and Savior, marvel at the mystery of the Triune God, and are deeply blessed and fed by the reading of Scripture, common prayer, and celebrations of baptism and the Lord's Supper. To this end, it is very helpful to pay attention to writings which seek to address a broad, trans-denominational spectrum. So perhaps you are a Protestant Christian who has never read a book by a Catholic writer, or a Catholic Christian who has never listened to a Catholic writer speaking in a broader trans-denominational conversation. Perhaps you live in a neighborhood with Protestant and Catholic neighbors who have never found a way to really talk together about matters of faith. Perhaps you are a pastor or leader who ministers among many people in these contexts. Perhaps you teach or learn in a college or seminary or other institution that draws together people from many denominations. May God's Spirit use your engagement with this book to strengthen your knowledge of and appreciation for the breadth of the church, and your own particular place in it.

And take note: one reason why a book like this can work so well across denominational lines is that it is saturated with references to and language drawn from the Bible (which you can quickly sense just by skimming the book and noticing all the parentheses!). Be sure to have a Bible nearby as you read this. If you make notes in your Bible of the texts mentioned in this book, you'll discover how the richest, deepest worship practices both express and form us in the entire sweep of biblical teaching.

JOHN D. WITVLIET
Calvin Institute of Christian Worship
Calvin College and Calvin Theological Seminary
Grand Rapids, Michigan

Introduction

When we hear the word "theologian," either we have no idea at all what the word means, or we think of our clergy person, or we recall a guest speaker we have heard during a retreat or renewal program, or we are reminded of a seminary professor we had, or we remember fondly the author of a favorite spiritual book. Most of us would hardly think of ourselves as theologians. After all, that term is left to the "God professionals." However, contrary to popular perceptions, as far as the origin of the word "theologian" is concerned, we are all theologians!

The word "theology" comes from the Greek (as is true of so much of our Christian language about worship because many of the early Christians were Greek-speaking), from two words meaning "God" (theo) and "word on" or "science of" (logos). Simply put, theology (informally, at least) is any talk about God. Any time we speak of our experiences of God — at worship during a shared reflection, in personal prayer, when overwhelmed by the beauty of nature, when moved by the generosity of people, when sharing with another some deep spiritual happening — we are doing theology. Yes, we faith-filled people are all truly theologians. We desire to talk about God. We hunger to understand God better and grow in our relationship with God. Various kinds of encounters with God (for example, at worship, while on a leisurely stroll, when in need) tend to well up in us, and the deeper the encounter, the deeper is the need to share the experience with others. That sharing is an important kind of theology. As we learn to speak about God, we come to know God better, desire God more, live God's will more faithfully.

We do talk about God! We are like Jeremiah: we encounter God and we cannot keep quiet about it (cf. Jer. 20:9). The more overwhelming the experience, the deeper the encounter, the more are we eager to share our God experience with someone who we believe will understand. We seek spiritual companions to whom we can talk about God and our spiritual growth. This kind of everyday God-talk is an important kind of theology. It forms us in our image of God, how we desire to worship, and how we address God in prayer. As many professional theologians have said, it is "first theology" — a theology that comes from deep within the heart, a theology that arises from experience, a theology that is a gift from a Triune God who desires to encounter us and be one with us.

This book arises from first theology — out of experiences of God and our talk about it — but its written form is "second theology." This other kind of theology is a further reflection on first theology. Second theology tries to make some kind of systematic sense out of a certain body of data about God. So, in one way or another, all theology — first (encounter and sharing) and second (reflection and systematizing) — begins with God and our experience of God. Both kinds of theology are essential. Without an experience or an encounter with God, we would have nothing to say about God.

Some raw data for this book (both first and second theology) as well as the impetus for its being written have been gleaned from several years of grant proposals submitted to the Calvin Institute of Christian Worship (CICW) for their Vital Worship Grants Program; I have studied these proposals as a member of the Vital Worship Grants Program Advisory Board. The grant proposal itself consists of a number of questions which applicants are to answer succinctly with respect to their proposals. One question in particular, concerned with describing Christian worship, has always caught my attention because the responses vary so greatly.

Part of the variation, to be sure, comes from the breadth of the Vital Worship Grants Program; each applicant has received his or her own denominational or communion formation while seeking an understanding of worship. Grants are accepted from any Christian denomination or tradition. But after reading hundreds of grants over the many years I have served on the Advisory Board, I have become increasingly fascinated by what I read between the lines of the responses to this all-important question directed at teasing out an understanding of worship.

I have detected struggle with the question. Some of the struggle may well be very practical: how to answer the question to support the grant request and impress the Grants Program Advisory Board. But I think something more credit-worthy and interesting is really at work. There is a struggle to answer succinctly a question about what worship is because Christian worship, first, has so many, many facets to it. Boiling it down to a single definition or short description seems to rob "worship" of its depth and richness. It seems to rob "worship" of its mystery, and we have a natural sense that no matter how much we do worship or how much we talk about it, we will never exhaust its possibilities, meanings, invitations, challenges, and consolations.

There is, of course, the Christian worship that is communal, well prepared (to a large extent "orchestrated"), and periodic (usually on Sunday). This communal, formal worship is most often a "given." It is carefully prepared, but usually only by a small part of the staff or congregation. Many congregations have specific programs that seek to involve more people in the worship preparation process (and we have received many written grants to this end). This issue frequently comes up when there is a felt desire to make the worship more multicultural, or more intergenerational, or more Scripture-based, or whatever is the felt need in the congregation for bettering the worship celebration.

There is also the worship that is less formal, hopefully undertaken more often throughout each day of the week, sometimes involving intentional prayer. But at other times this kind of informal worship is simply a spontaneous response of praise and gratitude for God's presence and goodness. "Thank you, God, for the good doctor's report." "O my dear God, I praise you for the beauty of this flower that has just opened up in my garden." "Glory to you, O Lord, for the beauty of these generous people who have responded to help the family who lost their home in a fire." "We rejoice, generous God, in the graciousness of your gifts of abundant food that we share in this meal." "Thank you, O good God, for helping me finish this task so well." "I lift my heart in deep gratitude, dear Lord, for finding out what is making my parent so ill."

I also think we struggle to answer a question about describing Christian worship because of the "worship climate" in both our churches and our society. Being used to having things largely our own way and according to our own preferences, it is difficult to give over to others something so important to us as worship. It is no secret that "worship wars" abound in many denominations or communions or independent churches. We struggle to find common ground for expressing together our praise and thanksgiving to God. Some churches have fixed texts or orders of service to which they adhere rather faithfully for structuring what they say in worship and how they go about thanking and praising God. Other churches have fixed texts or orders of service that serve only as guidelines, and they use these when they serve the immediate needs of the congregants but set them aside when there is a sense that other words or another structure better serves the folks in the pews or chairs. Still other churches have no fixed texts or order of service whatsoever, and each worship service is as creative and original as the planners can be, with changes coming as often as the imagination allows. And yet other churches have worship that is primarily spontaneous, with no pre-arranged agenda for the service whatsoever. Finding some common thread of understanding for what worship is in these diverse patterns of worship events is challenging indeed!

We sometimes struggle with Christian worship because we personally feel pulled in different directions. We want to experience (encounter) God in a strong, affective way; yet this does not always happen. This then raises important questions: Is worship directed only to God? Is it often subtly focused on us and our affective needs? What would a balanced combination of God and us look like during worship? This struggle has enormous implications for worship leadership; music in worship; enculturation issues; the prophetic or "feel good" content of preaching; the balance of vocal and silent times during worship; the proportion of personal and communal prayer; the ratio of prayers of praise, adoration, thanksgiving, and petition. *Worship with Gladness: Understanding Worship from the Heart* addresses these matters and much more.

Chapter 1 includes a consideration of what is happening in worship in our North American society today. Is worship being relegated to the periphery of our lives? What about the issue of formal, corporate worship as opposed to an individual walk in the woods to encounter God? Especially many young people would prefer to take this latter approach rather than to embrace any affiliation with organized religion. Are we perhaps, as a society, becoming more spiritual but less "religious"?

These and many similar questions are addressed, using an analysis of several hundred responses to the Vital Worship Grants Program proposal question about Christian worship. This review of grant proposals is a starting point for our reflections on worship; it is undertaken as a way to make explicit some trends in thinking about worship across denominational lines. It is not intended to be a statistical report; hence, there is no appendix to this book with tabulation results. This is partly to assure anonymity for the grant writers, and partly because the grants are so varied that it is well nigh impossible to categorize responses. What the analysis does do for us, however, is provide raw data for an initial theological reflection about worship, data that are grounded in actual worship experience, data that were not offered with this book in mind (hence, somewhat objective and unbiased as far as this book is concerned), and data that are broad and ecumenical in scope. The data enable us to locate challenges, commonalities, and divergences with respect to a Christian understanding of worship.

Chapter 2 delves into some of the rich data that Sacred Scripture, the Word of God, affords us in coming to a deeper understanding of worship over thousands of years of the Judeo-Christian tradition. It includes a close look at the fundamental commandment to worship God, an analysis of different genres of psalms to see what they can say to us about worship, and a consideration of Gospel texts and the heavenly worship as discovered in Revelation (the last book of the Christian Scriptures). The psalms are almost universally used in Christian worshiping communities. They are the prayer of Jesus himself. Psalm 100, I believe, can be a kind of "measure" for a basic understanding of the elements of Christian worship.

Against this basic understanding of worship gleaned from Scripture we compare the data and reflection from Chapter 1. The purpose is to come to an understanding about Christian worship that is comfortable for a wide spectrum of worshiping Christians and to promote conversations about worship across a wide spectrum of denominational boundaries. There is no "conversion" agenda in this book. The intent is not to bring readers to a single, common understanding of worship. Rather, we seek to find common ground for a worship understanding that is both challenging and affirming. Sometimes discussions across denominational boundaries point only to differences; this book points to what is common to all of us who choose to follow Jesus Christ as his faithful disciples. It attempts to appeal to a wide range of Christians through its trans-denominational lens.

Chapter 3 shifts from the "what" of worship to the "who" of worship and challenges each of us to deepen our quest for grasping the nature of Christian worship. Beginning with our common baptismal identity, this chapter underscores how our very Christian identity shapes and determines Christian worship. Part of the discussion is enriched from another source for principles of Christian worship, the Constitution on the Sacred Liturgy (*Sacrosanctum Concilium*), one of the constitutions of the Second Vatican Council. This was a Roman Catholic denominational event that quickly became a world-involving event that many other Christians came to appreciate. For the first time ever, observers who were not Roman Catholics were invited to be present at council sessions. Because the sixteen documents of Vatican II are a blueprint for religious renewal for the twenty-first century and include basic principles not only for worship renewal in the Catholic Church but also for the engagement of all the Christian churches in the challenges of the modern world, these documents have been studied and internalized by many more of the baptized than those confirmed in the Roman Catholic Church. It is a valuable resource for all of us for coming to understand worship more deeply.

Chapter 4 moves worship beyond the four walls of a church or meeting space to the domestic church, the church of everyday living. At stake in this chapter is coming to a greater appreciation for the relationship between Christian worship and authentic Christian living. Worship that stays in the building or sacred space is not really worship at all. If we are serious about giving our Triune God praise, adoration, and thanksgiving and are confident that our petitions are heard and answered (albeit not necessarily in the way

we think), then this becomes a way of life — a *spirituality*, if you
will. The truth of worship rests in the converging of word and deed
in our daily living. Our worship is more than a celebration service;
it is the expression of a *lived* spirituality, a way of life informing
everything we do, every decision we make, every relationship we
have. Every day and everything we do during the seeming ordinari-
ness of living can become acts of worship. What we do together
as a gathered Christian assembly for a few minutes or hours on
Sunday is a microcosm of who we are and how we are to live. The
gospel is ultimately the blueprint for daily living. Jesus' life, his
faithfulness to his Father's will, and the ever-so-gentle promptings
of the Holy Spirit are what truly define who we are and how we are.
God's Life-Spirit dwells within us as a lifeline to divine encounter
and gospel living. The Holy Spirit helps us understand worship
from our hearts.

Finally, the conclusion of this book attempts to answer what
the Grants question asks: "How would you describe Christian worship?" It also highlights the challenges that a fuller understanding
of the nature of worship brings.

Scattered throughout each chapter, ending each major subsec-
tion, is a feature called "Reflecting Pause." Every one of these is
an intended stopping point for the reader — a time to assess what
is being discussed and become aware if the text is challenging us,
and a time to pray about how this might lead us to worship better.
In this way, this book can also become a kind of personal "worship
journal," something we would want to come back to again and
again as a measure of our own moving forward in our appreciation
of worship and a way to assess our own personal worship needs.
This feature also makes the book ideal for study groups, who can
share reflections on what is, really, the most important aspect of
our Christian living: faithful and fruitful worship.

These reflections also say something about for whom this book

8

is intended: not specifically for the worship "professionals," but for anyone who desires to worship from the heart with greater understanding of what this important part of our days and weeks and years is all about. *Worship with Gladness: Understanding Worship from the Heart* might be a fitting supplementary text for a seminary or college/university class on worship, a good study text for worship preparation committees, and a resource for pastors wishing to continue their worship education and formation. An interesting phenomenon all denominations are facing these days is that more and more congregants are not "cradle" members. Churches now have members who grew up in and were formed in other denominations. For these folks, learning more about worship in general could be invaluable. Because this book is intended to appeal across denominational boundaries, specific aspects of particular denominational worship are not addressed. Rather, common elements consistent with any worship tradition are considered.

It has been a privilege and a marvelously stretching experience for me to have served on the Calvin Institute of Christian Worship Grants Advisory Board for a good number of years now. I have come to appreciate the many ways we can lift our hearts and minds to God in prayer, the beauty and importance of community, the great desire by a great number of people to improve how they give God praise and thanks. I am grateful to the good folks at Calvin College for this opportunity to serve the Christian churches. It is a fine example of how I receive far more than I give. And is not this true for all worship?

CHAPTER 1

Worship: Withering or Greening?

All people that on earth do dwell,
Sing to the Lord with cheerful voice;
Him serve with mirth, his praise forth tell;
Come ye before him and rejoice.

William Kethe, "All People That on Earth Do Dwell," verse 1

The Issue: What, Really, Is Worship?

Worship is much easier to celebrate than to describe! Worship is much easier to describe than to define! Once we move beyond the "givens," we often do not have a whole lot to say about worship. And yet, deep down, we all know when worship satisfies us or when worship leaves us feeling empty, when we hunger for more in worship or when we know we need to change how we worship.

One reason why worship in itself is so difficult to grasp is because there are so many variations on what worship is. When we visit other churches and participate in their services, we are comfortable with what is familiar to us from our own tradition, but we tend to be a bit uncomfortable with the unfamiliar. We may be fascinated by what is creative, new, or different, but fidelity to regular worship requires that we participate enough in a worship style or element that it is internalized, becomes comfortable and familiar. The reason for this need for "ownership" of worship is that without it worship can easily become focused on itself: on what we are doing, on how the elements are structured, on what is missing, on the relative importance or novelty of this or that element.

Another reason why worship is a knotty issue is because the Triune God we worship is not like us. Even Jesus, who became incarnate and dwelled among us (John 1:14) and was like us in all things except sin (2 Cor. 5:21), still was God. He had the power in the Spirit to heal, forgive, command nature, multiply bread and fishes, change water into wine, expel demons, raise the dead. If our understanding of God is as the divine One who is far away, judgmental, or demanding, our worship will reflect this. It will be difficult to find solace and satisfaction in worship. Worship will tend to be directed to placating such an exacting God or bargaining for what we need, but all with a sense of our own diminishment. Worship will be more duty than delight. On the other hand, if we experience God as the divine One who is compassionate and caring, loving and patient, kind and merciful, our worship will reflect this kind of relationship. We will approach worship with expectations and enthusiasm, assurance of forgiveness and help, and confidence that God hears us and answers our prayers. This worship is nothing less than a mutual exchange of love. This worship is pure joy, grace-filled, freeing.

A third reason that worship can be so hard to grasp is that so much of our society around us seems to hold devout people hostage. Sunday as a day of rest spent with family and friends seems to be all but lost for too many people. Shopping is a big culprit here, and we enable it by choosing to be in the "big box" stores and malls. Because of such activities, those who must work on Sunday and be away from family are not limited to emergency and helping professions (firefighters, police, doctors, nurses, social workers, etc.); now store managers and salesclerks are required to be on duty. Family prayer often took place at family mealtime, but packed schedules pulling us in many directions in so many cases force us to grab fast food on the run to the next activity. When both parents work long hours, it leaves them little quality time at home with each other, let alone with their children. The elderly are forgotten, and the values that naturally get passed on with the younger generations rubbing shoulders often with the older generations are too frequently lost.

Much has been said about our present "entitlement" generation, and this, too, can militate against a good worship ethic. If I expect everything about my life to revolve around me, and I expect to receive without any cost or consequences whatever I wish to have at the moment, then it is difficult to switch gears and surrender myself to Someone larger than myself outside of myself. Worship always involves giving myself — and my pleasures, needs, desires — over to something and Someone bigger than myself. If the universe revolves around my whims and wants, then it will be very difficult for me to adjust to any call to worship.

Yet another reason for our confusion about worship is that, subconsciously, we have so many other gods demanding our time, attention, and affection. Sports certainly would rank high on this list. Ball games (local, collegiate, and professional) now are sometimes scheduled on Sunday mornings, a traditional church time for Christians. Even Christmas and Easter are not exempt from the ubiquitous sporting events. Not too many years ago, Cincinnati, Ohio, was faced with an interesting dilemma. Traditionally the home of the first major league game of the baseball season (because that is where the first professional team was formed), first-game day in that city is always celebrated with a large parade and great festivities. One year, first-game day fell on Good Friday, and this coincidence precipitated a huge debate in the media. How could the tradition of first-game day be broken? Thankfully, this sacred day for Christians won the day! It was decided that the game would be played on Friday as scheduled, but the parade and festivities would be moved to Thursday. The very fact that such a debate arose (schedules are made out months ahead of time, and "Good Friday" probably escaped the schedulers) and lasted for as long as it did indicated something good. The people of Cincinnati somehow sensed that it was not quite right to have revelry on the very day we commemorate Jesus' suffering and death on the cross. The sports-god temptation includes such a diversity of pulls as golf tee times, Sunday-morning football analysis programs, and practice times scheduled in overbooked facilities. Part of the difficulty here is that sports can be wholesome activities involving exercise, learning team effort, travel, gleeful release, and so on. In themselves, sports are certainly not bad. But when sports become the center of our lives, and especially when sports get in the way of quality worship time, then something is amiss.

Another god militating against our deep internalization of worship, especially Sunday worship, is our own busy lives. By the time we get to Sunday, still a day when most of us do not have to get up to go to work, we are absolutely exhausted. We may party hard and late on Saturday night, and when we do finally fall into bed, our last thought is Good — I don't have to get up to my alarm clock tomorrow; I can sleep in. The thought of setting an alarm, getting up before we are completely rested or ready, dressing up for an important occasion, and getting to church is just too much for us to bear. It certainly is much easier to sleep in than make the effort to get to worship.

Finally, worship is sometimes hard to understand because it is poorly done, is too much of a contrast to our noisy lives, or challenges us and our way of living so that we are faced with needing to change or remaining uncomfortable with ourselves. Once we get into lifestyle patterns, it is very difficult to change them. Worship itself can become a lifestyle — in terms of setting aside regular, quality time to be at church with others, as well as oftentimes during the day turning our hearts and thoughts toward God. But for this to happen, it takes work on our part, a good bit of the effort literally being a choice to be countercultural. Many of us seem to be on a freight train on a fast track to nowhere. Worship calls us to slow down, quiet down, and set our priorities straight. Unless we consciously choose to do this, worship will wither away, not only in our own lives but essentially in society as a whole. Change is always costly. We must give up something in order to gain something we believe is better. And good worship always challenges us to change, to be transformed. Worship leaves us different, or it is not doing what it is supposed to do. The "different" is that we are more closely aligned with God — our will to the divine will. We are more deeply into a loving relationship with God — offering our imperfect human love in response to the divine overtures of perfect, unfailing love.

In spite of all this seeming withering of worship, we must be careful that we do not get too negative about what people do or don't do, how often they attend services, or what seem to be attitudes about worship among the majority. One of the temptations in evaluating worship and worship-like church activities is that we place a great deal of emphasis on numbers. And, of course, this is natural. Who wouldn't be pleased when, having planned a church formation program to study the Gospel of St. Mark, several hundred people show up the first night? Who wouldn't be pleased to have attendance at Sunday services equal attendance at the local high school's state championship football game? Who wouldn't be pleased to have the weekly Bible study group mushroom into a dozen energetic groups? Numbers are easily calculated. But they do not tell the whole story.

God obviously does not act on sheer numbers alone. Consider Abraham's bargaining with God (Gen. 18:22-33). Sodom and Gomorrah had become cities filled with people with "very grave sin." So Abraham begs God to spare the cities if there are fifty righteous people (that is, in right relationship with God and each other) living there. God agrees. Then Abraham bargains for the cities' salvation if forty righteous people can be found. Then thirty. Then twenty. Then ten. In all cases, God agrees. How bold is Abraham! How relenting and yielding is God! The story in Genesis stops with ten righteous people, and Sodom and Gomorrah are destroyed. Hm. Supposing Abraham had kept bargaining? Could he have worn God down to relenting divine punishment for only one righteous person? Genesis does not give us the answer, but Jesus does. All of Chapter 15 in Luke's Gospel is an answer, for there we find the three great parables of mercy: the shepherd who leaves ninety-nine sheep to go find the one lost (not a very good economic gamble, but a great loving risk); the woman who wastes lamp oil looking, energy sweeping, and time searching to find one coin out of ten she loses (not a very good return on personal expenditure, but a great joy in the finding); and the prodigal father who not only takes back his wayward son but runs out to meet him, kisses him, clothes him in a garment worthy of an heir, bestows jewelry on him, and throws a feast (not a very good way to keep proper hierarchy in the household, but a great fatherly relating). No, God is not very concerned with numbers alone. God desires only that in our worship we open our lips to declare divine praises (Ps. 51:15) and that we offer God our very selves in service of others:

> "With what shall I come before the LORD,
>   and bow myself before God on high?
> Shall I come before him with burnt offerings,
>   with calves a year old?

Will the LORD *be pleased with thousands of rams,*
   with ten thousand of rivers of oil?
Shall I give my firstborn for my transgression,
   the fruit of my body for the sin of my soul?"
He has told you, O mortal, what is good;
   and what does the LORD *require of you*
but to do justice, and to love kindness,
   and to walk humbly with your God? (Mic. 6:6-8)

This kind of worship — emulating God's care and largesse toward us — has a common echo in the prophets. Amos says something very similar to what Micah does (Amos 5:21-24). Hosea says it quite succinctly: "For I desire steadfast love and not sacrifice, the knowledge of God rather than burnt offerings" (Hos. 6:6).

There are many positive signs in our society that worship is still quite healthy, that our worship is in a constant process of greening. Our country is a world leader in philanthropy — and not just the kind of aid given by the government (which often is motivated by politics and self-interest). Private foundations and individuals are most generous when needs arise. When a natural disaster strikes, for example, not only do we donate money, but countless people drop their own everyday lives and travel many miles to pitch in personally with whatever cleaning up and rebuilding are necessary and helpful. All of these kinds of gracious acts often flow from sincere worship as a lifestyle. These acts of justice and kindness, as the prophets tell us, are truly worship.

Another sign of the greening of worship is that, time and again, efforts to remove our national motto "In God we trust" from our coins and our civil-institution facades have failed. Although prayer is no longer allowed in our public schools as part of the daily schedule, some young people gather on their own to pray. Banning prayer at presidential inaugurations has never taken hold in any formal or large way. While opinion polls many times report the demise of religion in our country, what is surveyed has more to do with organized religion (which has not always done things in ways to keep a very good name for itself) and less to do with a lifestyle of spirituality and worship. We like to tenaciously hang onto the fact that our country was founded on religious principles, founded by people fleeing from countries where they could not worship freely, founded on the belief that to be a successful democracy we must adhere to God's laws before we make our own laws.

Many other factors figure into the withering and greening of worship. Cost of congregation plants, issues around generational differences, economics, social status, traditions, past hurts and disappointments, availability of leadership and proper formation, and many other considerations shape how we think about worship, how we embrace worship, and how much we desire worship. So, in terms of the question "What, really, is worship?" we find a simple answer not so easy to offer. Perhaps it is better that we neither define nor even describe it, but that we learn better how to *do* it. Basic to fidelity to regular worship is a *good experience* of worship. What best calls us to worship is a felt need to surrender ourselves to God's presence, a felt need that essentially arises out of a *good experience* of worship.

This last statement is often clearly borne out at crisis moments in our lives. When a loved one dies, we need a pastor's wisdom and a congregation's comfort. We tend to fall back on our memory of an earlier experience of the kind of peace and comfort that worship can bring. When we are ready to marry, we are often dissatisfied with simply a civil ceremony; we have a sense that making a lifetime commitment to another person is a sacred act and must be celebrated as such. When we lose a job or go bankrupt or are faced with a serious illness, out of a sense of our own powerlessness we turn to the God who has proven faithful. Those who live with only themselves to think about are often sad and lonely. Much is being written these days about social networks on the Internet, about how some people have thousands of "friends." Do they? Acquaintances or strangers are not friends. Friends are those who empathize with us in our sorrow or need and rejoice with us in our good fortune, who are present to us in good times and bad (see Sir. 6:5-17).

....

Reflecting Pause

In our congregation, we experience the greening of worship in . . .
We experience the withering of worship in . . .
Worship is most important to us when . . .
It is least important to us when . . .
We personally most feel the need to worship when . . .
We personally least feel the need to worship when . . .
At this point, our congregation would describe worship as . . .

....

A Clarification: Worship and/or Liturgy?

If we find it difficult to define or even accurately describe worship, the same is true for the term "liturgy." Often the two are used interchangeably, and there is no problem with this so long as the context helps us know about which we are speaking. Theologically, however, many professionals make a distinction. In our reflections in these chapters, I sometimes interchange the two words, and sometimes I use "worship" and "liturgy" as very distinct entities, with "liturgy" being a subset of the larger category of "worship." In fact, there is more than one sense for using the words "worship" and "liturgy." Again, it is context that helps us understand what we mean.

Worship, as intimated above, can be a very broad notion embracing many different kinds of activities. We can worship formally with others in church on Sunday. We can worship God in private moments when we take time out from our busy daily routine to lift our heart in thanks and praise or petition. We can worship God in a small group prayer, in Bible study, while driving to work or school, while on a leisurely walk in a park, during a brilliant and glorious sunrise or sunset, or while observing a tender and caring moment between a care giver and an elderly person. Any time we focus ourselves on God, we can be in a worship mode. So, while it is perhaps easiest to think of worship in more formal, church-service terms, in reality worship can be far broader than something defined by conventional practices. As any dictionary will tell, the etymology of "worship" probably comes from the Middle English meaning "worthy" or "worth" — the honor given God simply because God deserves, is worthy of, our honor, love, and allegiance.

Originally, "liturgy" has a narrower meaning, and so we can guess that theologically and in practice it has a narrower meaning as well. Coming from two Greek words meaning "work of the people," "liturgy" originally referred to public service by some for the good of all. Liturgy is a formulary for worship, a particular way of doing public worship. While the church's liturgy began as a common effort within the whole Christian community (see Acts 2:43-47), it eventually devolved to an action performed by a minister on behalf of the people. Liturgy became exclusively and narrowly understood as the performance of rituals. This is one part of the climate during the Reformation that the early Reformers sought to redress. It is good for us to revisit the nature of worship and liturgy now, these many centuries later.

While all liturgy is worship (or should be!), not all worship is liturgy (from a narrower, theological understanding). In other words, liturgy is a subcategory of worship. For us Christians, it is a response to Jesus' command at the Last Supper to "Do this in remembrance of me" (Luke 22:19). Thus, one qualifying feature of Christian liturgy is that it derives from the life and ministry of Jesus himself and is a response to his command. In a real way it continues Jesus' saving ministry. Liturgy makes present the life, saving mission, suffering and death, and resurrection and ascension of Jesus, as well as the sending of the Spirit and the inauguration of the church. In short, it celebrates and makes present the whole saving mystery of Jesus Christ. The liturgical movement of the twentieth century, concerned with worship/liturgical renewal, tended to refer to this saving mystery of Christ as the "paschal mystery." It celebrates Jesus' passing over from death to life and our own share in that passing over (see Romans 6).

For some congregations, the distinction between worship and liturgy might not be applicable or even helpful. For others, this distinction might sharpen how a congregation wishes to renew its worship. For still others, the distinction might affirm commitments and practices already in place. That said, one easy way to approach similarities and differences between worship and liturgy is to chart twelve characteristics of each side by side on a table with two columns (see p. 22). Following the table are comments on the various comparative characteristics.

Before reflecting further on these distinctions, let us consider some aspects common to both worship and liturgy. Christian worship and liturgy both are directed to God rather than ourselves. God is at the center of worship and liturgy. Further, the purpose of both is other-centered — that is, worship and liturgy lead us to be concerned about others, to care for others, to love others more deeply. Both are personal — that is, they both require of us a conscious surrender to the prayer taking place. We must be present to the prayer and celebration. No one can do worship or liturgy for us. For this reason — both are personal — culture plays a big part

Two Approaches to Christian Assembling

Worship (Devotional, Expressive)	Liturgy (Ritualized, Formative)
Open in style; changing to meet various needs	Largely given structures and texts
Familiar, comfortable service, often less formal leadership	Formal, distinct ritual; designated leadership
Possibly communal, but not necessarily so	Necessarily communal
Is unlimited in themes and styles	Is focused on themes of Jesus' saving work (paschal mystery)
Fluid interchange of select worship elements	A rhythm of word and sign
Can focus on individuals or local congregation	Directs local community to the larger church
Is creative, open-ended, often very contemporary	Embodies a long tradition of celebration
Local congregation may be unique in worship style	Liturgy involves shared worship style with other congregations
Service is shaped locally	Service is shaped by tradition of ritual
May focus on individual needs	Is directed to needs of larger church and world
Involves a wide range of emotions	Involves varying emotions throughout the liturgical year
May focus on a specific Person of the Trinity	Is Trinitarian in shape and celebration

in both worship and liturgy. We come to worship and liturgy with who we are. We do not set aside our family backgrounds, contexts, and values. Cultural expression requires more than singing a hymn in another language or choosing ethnic music. Enculturated prayer comes from deep within the identity of an individual, and is shared by all those who hail from the same country or region, those with a shared culture. Many of our church congregations now represent many peoples of many different cultures, and it is very challenging to find ways to worship or do liturgy together with such diversity, respecting and embodying differences yet at the same time searching for our common ground before the one God we acclaim.

Now, to turn to the differences from our table above. One of the most noticeable distinctions between worship and liturgy concerns the use of given structures and texts. We usually refer to "liturgical tradition churches" as those which have clear worship guidelines and authoritative texts. Some churches have service books with fixed texts, but those texts are essentially guidelines and may be freely adapted. Other churches have service books with fixed texts that are givens and may be adapted in only limited fashion. Still other churches have no common tradition, no fixed texts, and no specific criteria for their worship. The advantage of fixed texts is that individual wants and needs are less likely to creep into the service. Fixed texts structurally capture the theology of worship of the congregation. Fixed texts are more easily identifiable among various congregations of the same tradition. The advantage of open-style services without fixed texts is that they more easily meet contemporary needs, with people finding themselves and their own lives more surely reflected in the service. The service can be quite creative and imaginative, especially capturing the free-flowing imaginations and need for creativity (read as "not boring") of the younger members of the congregation.

Because worship is so broad in its application, there are more possibilities for it to be familiar and comfortable, with less formal leadership. While it is true that most congregations have duly prepared and ordained ministers presiding over Sunday worship, these worship leaders are not essential for all forms of worship. A small group of individuals can gather to worship, and individuals certainly worship God in their personal prayer. This kind of prayer lends itself to a greater sense of community among the body of worshipers (if the worship is communal). The space can be a more comfortable one, with worshipers sitting around on couches and in easy chairs. Many independent house churches are very familiar with this kind of communal worship. Liturgy, on the other hand, is necessarily more formal, follows a distinct ritual pattern, and has a clear hierarchy of ministers, including not only the worship leader but also other recognized worship ministers such as elders and/ or deacons, lay readers, the psalmist or cantor, ushers, preachers, and so on.

Worship may be communal, with either a large or small number of people making up the congregation, but worship need not necessarily be communal. As said above, we can worship alone in the privacy of our homes or bedrooms, in a hospital room or a hotel room — even on a ball field. Liturgy, however, is necessarily communal not only because liturgy belongs to the domain of the whole church and is a celebration of the whole church, but also because the very gathering of the people for liturgy makes present the church, the Body of Christ. Individually we are members of the Body of Christ, but when we come together for the express purpose of celebrating liturgy to enact the mystery of salvation revealed to us, we are no longer simply *members* of the Body; we surrender our own selves to *be* the Body along with all others who are present. Liturgy is a visible expression of Jesus' promise that "where two or three are gathered in my name, I am there among them" (Matt. 18:20).

Worship can be unlimited in themes and styles and can focus much more easily on contemporary events. This is one reason why denominations with a strong liturgical tradition often schedule communal worship in addition to the regularly scheduled liturgies. For example, in January, on or near the feast of the conversion of St. Paul (January 25), there are often ecumenical worship services in which prayers are offered for Christian unity. Or during times of national crisis (such as 9/11 or Hurricane Katrina or Hurricane Sandy), congregations will often schedule prayer gatherings around these particular events. All of this is an essential expression of our care and love for each other; it is all part of being members of the one family of God. While prayers during a liturgy (for example, the Lord's Supper) might mention such crises, and there would very appropriately be intercessory prayer sometime during the liturgy that kept in mind the hardship of the people affected by these disasters, this kind of prayer is not the primary intent of liturgy. Rather, Christian liturgy celebrates and in theme or intent is limited to the kind of structured prayer that makes present Jesus' saving work. Liturgy enacts the divine economy of salvation. In a sense, then, worship is more open to immediate needs; liturgy is more open to the larger issue of how we continue Jesus' saving work in the here and now.

Since worship does not necessarily require fixed texts and set structures, there can be a fluid interchange of select worship elements. Not every worship service would have the same elements arranged in the same way. This is especially true when the worship event is not a regular Sunday-morning service. On the contrary, liturgy usually includes a rhythm of word and sign (sacrament), in that order. The word proclaimed and preached is the context for and gives particular meaning on this day to the sacramental action. In this regard, music is a special consideration. In worship the music itself can be the text and structure of the worship. So some church services include a great deal of music, movement, and acclamatory utterances. The Spirit is given rather free rein to influence worshipers and move them to praise. In liturgy, music is important, but it is not a central element. The music serves the ritual action (such as accompanying a procession), or the music may well be sung liturgical text (such as the *Kyrie, Gloria, Sanctus,* or *Agnus Dei*).

Worship's breadth leaves a great deal of room for it to focus on individuals or local congregations. So it is entirely appropriate during worship to hear about what the little ones have learned during Sunday school, what the adolescents have learned from their latest service project, and what the needs of the nearest food pantry are. Worship is not simply a town-hall meeting, but it does have room in its open structure to experience how concern for others is a way to give God praise and thanksgiving.

One of the repeated injunctions of the Hebrew Scriptures is that God's people care for "the alien, the orphan, and the widow" (see, for example, Deut. 24:19-21). These were disenfranchised groups in the Israelite community who had no way to take care of themselves: the alien was a sojourner in a foreign land with no rights; the orphan had no parents to care for him or her; the widow had no husband to support her. God clearly gives a reason for this care:

> You shall not wrong or oppress a resident alien, for you were aliens in the land of Egypt. You shall not abuse any widow or orphan. If you do abuse them, when they cry out to me, I will surely heed their cry; my wrath will burn, and I will kill you with the sword, and your wives shall become widows and your children orphans. (Exod. 22:21-24)

At first hearing this may sound harsh to our ears, but God is basically saying that we are to treat each other as God has already treated us. God has given us freedom and all good things for our care; in turn, we are to be concerned for others who have less than we do and are in need. When care for others is part of the shape of worship itself (in the early church the gifts brought to the altar were largely gifts for the poor), this care itself is a most sublime act of worship because we are acting toward others in the way that God has acted toward us. Liturgy is also always concerned with the needs of people, addressed structurally in the presentation of gifts and intercessory prayer. These gifts and prayers are generally for local needs. But the context of the giving is beyond the immediate locale and needs. The liturgical community is the whole church of Christ, and so gifts for one in a real way are gifts for all. As St. Paul reminds us, when we build up one member of the Body, we build up the whole Body (1 Cor. 12:14-27; cf. Eph. 4:12; 5:29-30).

Worship often is creative, open-ended, and very contemporary. Multimedia, radically different music styles, film, drama, art, and dance can all be effective tools leading the faithful to prayerful worship. In many churches, even Sunday services, which tend to be more formal, are quite different from week to week. The limits are only the imagination of the worship planners and the requirement that to be worship, whatever the creative endeavor is, it must have as its purpose leading the congregation to prayerful worship of God. Liturgy need not be boring and staid, but it is primarily faithful to a long tradition of celebration, which tends to shape (and to some extent limit) creativity in certain ways.

Local congregations might be quite unique in their worship styles, which may vary greatly from one congregation to the next, even within a single denomination. Liturgy, because of its given texts and structure, has a shared worship pattern with other congregations, especially within the same denomination. One of the marvelous fruits of Christian worship renewal largely precipitated by Vatican II, with its landmark Constitution on the Sacred Liturgy (previously mentioned), is the amount of texts shared among various Christian denominations. Service books have shared Great Thanksgivings and Eucharistic Prayers. The Roman Lectionary and the Common Lectionary are very similar, and so on any given Sunday the same readings are proclaimed and preached in myriad congregations across the country and even throughout the whole Christian world.

We might shape worship services. We are free to construct them in many ways, with different elements, with all the creativity we can muster. Our shaping worship means we are quite free to take into account local circumstances, special events, and urgent needs. On the other hand, liturgy, by its ritual structure, forms and transforms us. All ritual, by its very nature, transforms. For example, boys or girls begin a puberty rite as youth; they complete the rite and are recognized as adults. A man and a woman come to a wedding ceremony as individuals and leave as a couple where "they become one flesh" (Gen. 2:24). So it is with liturgy. The transformation may not be so clearly evident or startling as it is with some rituals, but God does transform those congregants who surrender themselves to the liturgical action. We leave liturgy changed, more perfectly members of Christ's Body equipped to continue Jesus' saving mission in whatever circumstances our daily life leads us. Liturgy equips us to be leaven in our broken world, to bring to it forgiveness and healing. Of course, worship might also form and transform individuals. And good worship probably does. The difference here lies in the structure: the very structure of liturgy as ritual has as one of it purposes transformation of those given over to the liturgy.

Worship may rightly focus on individual needs. There may be an altar call when someone might publicly profess conversion. There may be witness talks or testimonies when congregants share how God has worked in their lives. There may be pleas for help, mercy, guidance, inclusion, understanding. The congregation celebrating liturgy surely would not want to be impervious to such individual needs, but they would generally not be individually expressed within the shape of the liturgy itself. Instead, the prayers and concerns during liturgy are directed to needs of the whole church and world because the Body of Christ comprises the whole church and world. This point makes clear that liturgical prayer cannot be the only kind of prayer for congregations with a liturgical tradition. Every congregation needs worship prayer that carries them outside of themselves in concrete expression of care for others. This makes clear that worship and liturgy are never mutually exclusive. Liturgical traditions need time for worship services that express individual needs and that also assure one of God's and the congregation's care and presence and that what is happening in one's life matters.

Worship generally involves a broad range of expressed emotions, determined only by the choices made or the order of service on a given day. Liturgical prayer, on the other hand, gives expression to varying emotions throughout the liturgical year. The weight of expressing various emotive stances does not fall on any one liturgy, but is spread throughout the unfolding of Jesus' life and ministry in the course of the liturgical year. Thus what immediately colors a liturgical service is where we are in the church year. Advent's expectation of Christ's presence (John 1:19-34), Christmas's joyful celebration of his birth in human flesh (John 1:14; Luke 2:10-11), Epiphany's homage (Matt. 2:10-11), Lent's call for conversion (Mark 1:12-15), Easter's glorious new life (John 20:14-18), Pentecost's power-filled gift (Acts 2:1-38), the Sundays after Pentecost (or Ordinary Time) with their challenge to walk with Jesus to Jerusalem and the cross, learning how to be faithful disciples (Luke 9:23-24, 51-53) — all these things are brought to life during liturgy, but most clearly during these particular times of the church year.

Worship may address one or another Person of the Trinity. Often charismatic worship is quite Spirit-filled, and the movement of the Spirit among the congregants is palpable. At other times worship may be directed to God the Father, especially if the theme of the day is creation and God's beneficence. At other times worship may well be about Christ's suffering and death and all that he willingly undertook for our salvation. Liturgical prayer, however, is always Trinitarian in shape and celebration. Following the patristic tradition, liturgy is ordinarily addressed to the Father, through the Son, in the Holy Spirit.

None of these comparisons are intended to convey a value judgment about whether worship or liturgy ought to be the service of the day for any given congregation. That is determined by church tradition and polity. Nor am I suggesting that we cannot continue to use worship and liturgy interchangeably, for we probably will. There is no right or wrong here. And congregational traditions must always be respected. However, it does move our understanding of worship forward when we have a grasp of the distinction between worship and liturgy.

....

Reflecting Pause

The element of distinction between worship and liturgy that
    strikes us as the most important for our congregation is ...
This distinction helps us make clear that ...
Our understanding of worship has moved forward in these
    ways ...
The Scripture reference that has most helped us understand wor-
    ship a little better is ...
At this point, our congregation would describe worship as ...

....

The Data: What Do We Say about Worship?

I have closely analyzed hundreds of Calvin Institute of Christian Worship grant proposals that were submitted over a four-year period, and read hundreds of others for about a decade. In particular, as I have mentioned, I have been interested in the question on the grant application that asks the prospective grantees to explain what, really, is worship. What intrigued me about this question (and became the germinating seed for this book exploring a theology of worship that crosses denominational lines) was its wording: "How would you describe Christian worship?" The responses were always rich and varied and provide an invaluable body of data for moving forward in an understanding of worship. But it was how often the grantees quoted John 4:24 — "God is spirit, and those who worship him must worship in spirit and truth" — that struck me so forcibly and eventually really intrigued me. This Scripture passage was given more than three times more often than any other response, even the response that worship gives God glory, praise, and thanks.

It took me years of reflection to finally come to the insight that I think explains this focus on John 4:24, and that is the wording of the question itself. Sometimes the way we phrase a question makes all the difference in the world in terms of what kind of an answer we get. In this case, the earlier formulation of the question on the grant proposal was "How would you describe authentic worship?" The word "authentic" became the most important word in the question and shaped so many of the earlier responses. Many respondents, I came to see, understood "authentic" as "true," and so this passage from John's Gospel was a good fit in response. What bothered me, however, is that a careful reading of this passage (which we do in the next chapter) suggests a different context and interpretation.

Once I had this insight, I suggested at an Advisory Board meeting that we change the way we phrase the question, leaving out the word "authentic." After all, the question is intended simply to help prospective grantees to measure their proposed worship renewal project against their understanding of worship. With the change of the question to "How would you describe Christian worship?" — leaving out the word "authentic," which seemed to throw everyone off — the responses changed greatly. I read far more thought and insight into the question, and the number of times John 4:24 was cited was reduced considerably.

Once the focus on John 4:24 was out of the picture, the responses to the question concerning an understanding of worship varied appreciably. Some responses resorted to the origin of the word "worship," meaning "to give worth." Most often the response referred to our giving God thanks, praise, and glory. Worship as being Spirit-filled was a common response of independent, free-church grant applicants, as was coming into God's presence. Encounter with God ranked high, parallel to coming into God's presence. As might be expected, once these common themes were tabulated, the responses covered scores of different attitudes and stances before God. I read responses that said worship is everything

- from duty to a means of grace;
- from a humbling of self to an encounter with and a growing in holiness;
- from outward expression of intense feelings to a lifestyle;
- from being in communion with each other to opening the soul to the wonder of God;
- from a public expression of faith to a response to God's unconditional love;
- from welcome, outreach, and service to a response to God's desire for unity;

- from not being tied to traditional practices to not being afraid to follow norms;
- from promoting a sense of well-being to responding to God's revelation;
- from relationship with God and one another to divine-human interaction;
- from sacrifice to speaking to and listening for God;
- from discovering the truth about God and self to a love relationship with an awesome God;
- from God-initiated and God-enabled to homage offered to God.

Every one of these statements says something important about worship; we can learn something from each of them. Most of all we learn that worship is a personal, rich, meaningful activity to which people are faithful out of love.

Many words kept recurring in the responses, and each of them can tell us something even more about worship. Some of the words and phrases that came up most frequently were these: "praise," "thanksgiving," "love," "encounter," "presence," "word and table," "response to God," "humility and homage," "communication," "reverence," and "communion/unity." A couple of surprises surfaced. One is that the paschal mystery (to be discussed more fully in Chapter 3), here-and-now made present during liturgy, was alluded to in different ways, such as "re-enacts Christ's redemptive activity." While most of the responses indicated a sense that worship is directed to "God" (within the context generally meaning the First Person of the Holy Trinity, the Creator), mention of the paschal mystery (using this phrase or other words identifying the same saving mystery) points to a strong sense that the Sunday service derives from Christ and his saving deeds (a point of distinction we made above with respect to worship and liturgy).

What also surprised me is that no response raised the issues of worship being boring, repetitive, out of touch with real life, hard to enter into, or not worth the time and effort put into doing it well. The overwhelmingly positive attitudes toward worship no doubt are partly due to the fact that the grant applicants are personally and heavily involved in worship planning and practices — many of them are ordained. But beneath this obvious point something else lies. There is an enthusiasm about worship and its effects on individuals and communities that can come only from personal commitment to quality worship and prayer. At a time when there seems to be a withering of worship among many people, these responses also show a greening of worship. People exhibit a real desire to grow in their understanding and practice of worship. Many responses clearly indicated concern that worship is not about us, but is essentially about our turning toward God. Social concerns were mentioned fairly frequently, but this was largely in the sense that worship naturally leads to care for others, a point made above.

Coupling the response to the question about the meaning of worship with the grant proposal question asking about bibliography, it also came clear to me that the understanding of worship was directly shaped by what the grantees read, who they heard as speakers, and what they did not read. This suggests that a well-rounded understanding of worship is best informed by reading a great variety of authors, from within one's tradition and outside it, from within one's worship comfort zone and outside it. If ongoing worship renewal is to happen, we must be willing to be stretched and be willing to learn from others who worship in a way different than we do.

Some other interesting points emerged from analyzing the grant proposals. Rarely was prayer itself mentioned, possibly because it was taken for granted that no matter how one approached worship, prayer is at its heart. Yet I think this premise might be examined. I have been to worship services where the sense of community, concern for others, and care for those in need was quite evident within the shape of the service itself, but actual time for prayer was very limited in terms of the whole worship service. So perhaps we need to consider prayer in worship as well as worship as prayer.

Often respondents went to *ways* to worship; we are more comfortable with the concrete than with the mystery that worship is. There was some concern with inclusivity, outreach, welcome, feeling at home, and expressing feelings during worship. Most of the respondents clearly understood that worship is in every way a search for God, a lifelong process. They also expressed concern that worship is directed to God, at the same time that community and fellowship among the congregants is very important.

Something else that emerges from these rich responses concerning the meaning of worship is that no one person has a complete answer. In worship we are dealing essentially with great mystery: how and why the Deity chooses to reveal the divine Self to us; that we are loved and forgiven in spite of our sinful disruptions in our halting relationship with God; the wondrous reality that God chose to take on human flesh and dwell among us as one of us; that the Spirit who dwells within us through baptism (developed in Chapter 3) transforms us and draws us closer to God; that God's glory is all around us and that our encounters with this illuminating divine presence feed our worship and make it ever richer; that our simple and humble prayers are truly answered (even if not quite in the way we expect or want); that God loves us so much that we are adorned with great beauty, fed with abundance beyond measure, and given dignity even above that of the angels (cf. Luke 12:7, 22-31; Ps. 8:5).

Is this not such a great mystery: worship turns our hearts toward God, but then we receive so much in return!

....

Reflecting Pause

The elements of worship with which we most easily identify are ...
The elements of worship that make us most uncomfortable are ...
List and ponder five words which might help congregants become more enthusiastic about their worship experience:
With respect to our experience of the Sunday service, we need to ...
What confuses us about worship is ... What encourages our congregation about worship is ...

....

Worship Needs: Are There Elements We Sometimes Forget?

When we think of worship, a number of elements common to just about every congregation's service come to mind: word, table, music, preaching, environment, gestures, posture, movement. Often multimedia equipment is used; sound systems are evident; candles are lit; vesture may be worn; choirs may be robed; children have a part. Many congregations make a concerted effort to welcome the disabled, the homeless, the seekers. Any one of these elements may actually be an occasion for worship, can lead us to prayer, can turn us toward God. A worship *service* emerges when some or all of these elements are configured in a meaningful way, with a progression to them that draws the congregants more deeply into an encounter with God.

We turn now to some elements that are part of worship, but perhaps are not used to the best advantage or understood in a broad enough way in some congregations. Other elements that we reflect on here may be lacking in most if not all worship services of any given congregation. The comments here do not imply that certain elements of worship *must* be used. But I hope that these comments will challenge worship planners to consider moving worship occasionally (always?) in a slightly different direction.

PRAYER

That worship is prayer no one would argue. But in practice, a question truly does arise: How much of our worship is actually prayer, and how much of our worship tends to have a different focus, even leading us away from prayer? Of course, it is not possible for us humans to spend very much time single-mindedly focused on God. We so easily become distracted with everything from "I forgot to get the meat for dinner out of the freezer" to "Where are we going to go for brunch after the service?" to "I wonder how Uncle Mike in the hospital is doing" to "When am I going to find a job?" to . . . fill in the blank! When such distractions occur (and they will, countless times during a service!), we must be gentle with ourselves, but at the same time firm. Sometimes it is good to arrive for a service early and deliberately catalog what most concerns us and then gently put each matter out of our mind for the time being. By bringing our concerns to consciousness, we can more easily set them aside. Sometimes, too, our concerns can become the focus of our prayer; if a family member is gravely ill, of course that will color all of our prayer.

Prayer is more than saying prayers, although it also is that. Jesus himself taught us how to pray (Matt. 6:9-13; Luke 11:2-4); the Our Father remains one of the most widely prayed and beloved Christian prayers of all time. Scriptures often show Jesus going off by himself to pray — sometimes going up on a mountain, a scriptural metaphor for coming close to God. Rarely do we know the content of Jesus' prayer, the one extended exception being Jesus' prayer for his disciples at the Last Supper as recorded in John's Gospel (John 17:1-26). Jesus' whole heart is turned toward his Father at the same time that he is so aware of the weakness and need of his followers. Such sensitivity and compassion the praying Jesus has! We do well to learn from him.

A very poignant example of Jesus' prayer is at the tomb of his friend Lazarus (John 11:28-44). Having arrived at the place where Lazarus is buried, "Jesus began to weep" (v. 35). This does not escape the bystanders, who remark on how much Jesus loved Lazarus (v. 36). After the stone has been rolled away from the opening of the tomb, we hear Jesus' prayer, and it is filled with utter confidence and trust: "Father, I thank you for having heard me. I knew that you always hear me . . ." (vv. 41b-42). This is surely a great lesson for our own prayer: Have confidence; God always hears us. Such tender love the praying Jesus has! We do well to learn from him.

The accounts of Jesus' final hours in Jerusalem before his death and resurrection are filled with heart-wrenching prayers that teach us surrender to God's will. Jesus' prayer in the Garden of Gethsemane is particularly telling and comforting for us when we face extreme difficulties. All three Synoptic Gospels let us glimpse a very human Jesus who is begging his Father to "let this cup pass from me" (Matt. 26:39; Mark 14:36; Luke 22:42). Jesus' prayer is intense; his request is a matter of life and death. Matthew and Mark both show the intensity of Jesus' desire to avoid his demise at the hands of his enemies by having Jesus repeat three times that this ordeal should pass from him.

Luke uses another image to depict the intensity of Jesus' prayer: "In his anguish he prayed more earnestly, and his sweat became like great drops of blood falling down on the ground" (Luke 22:44). In the Hebrew mind, blood was the seat of life. What Luke is portraying for us is that in Jesus' very struggle to surrender his will to the Father's will, his life was already being poured out. His "yes" to the Father was to surrender his life. Luke does not record Jesus' "yes" as does Matthew's "your will be done" (Matt. 26:42; cf. Matt. 6:10: "Your will be done," a petition in Matthew's version of the Our Father) and Mark's "yet, not what I want, but what you want" (Mark 14:36). Still, Luke's image of blood-sweat surely is a "yes" revealing the incredible cost of Jesus' fidelity. Such surrendering power the prayer of Jesus has! We do well to learn from him.

Even in Jesus' darkest hour, while he is hanging on the cross, there is prayer on Jesus' lips. Matthew and Mark show us a distraught and alone Jesus: "My God, my God, why have you forsaken me?" (Matt. 27:46; Mark 15:34). Luke shows us a forgiving Jesus (Luke 23:34), a compassionate Jesus with his promise-filled response to the Good Thief (Luke 23:43), and a willing Jesus as he gives himself back to the Father: "Father, into your hands I commend my spirit" (Luke 23:46). John shows us a caring Jesus as he commends his mother and beloved disciple John to each other (John 19:26-27). After this final loving act of a Son tying up loose ends, Jesus is free to utter "It is finished" (John 19:30). Such total surrender the prayer of Jesus has! We do well to learn from him.

Most likely none of us will ever face crucifixion for being followers of Jesus. Yet his prayer at this time of his greatest need can still be our prayer. What we learn from Jesus is that prayer is essentially a surrender of one's control, power, desires, needs, pleasures, and will into the hands of God, a surrender that results in union between pray-er and God. It is this union which Jesus constantly reveals to us in his prayer (cf. John 17:11). Prayer, then, may include words, but its intent and the deepest form of prayer itself do not need words. Prayer is simply union with God. Our prayer now is a foretaste of the eternal union that eternal life promises. And ultimately this is what keeps us faithful to prayer: that one day the union with our Triune God that brings so much joy and peace will be ours, effortlessly, for all eternity.

Spiritual traditions have taught different kinds of prayer: adoration, praise, thanksgiving, petition. Spiritual mentors have taught different ways to pray: meditation, contemplation, repetition. In the last analysis, all of this is directed toward the union with God which Jesus ceaselessly enjoyed and to which his very life and call beckon us. We sometimes make the mistake in our prayer that we can change God's "mind" about things. But God is immutable. We humans change. Prayer changes us. Prayer changes us in such a way that we hunger more deeply for the kind of union Jesus always enjoyed with his Father. Both personal prayer and corporate worship beckon us to seek this union, to hunger for this union, and to celebrate this union with God.

PROFESSION

Earliest baptismal evidence shows us that a profession of faith has always been an essential element of baptism. Often we focus more on the renunciation of sin as a primary baptismal act. In some early church communities this was profoundly indicated by the candidates' turning from the west (the region of darkness and sin) to the east (the region of light and Life). Yes, rejection of evil is essential for anyone who wishes to follow Christ. But rejection — essentially a negative act — is not enough. Rejection must be followed by an adherence to something (Someone) else. This adherence is expressed by a common creedal statement, a synopsis of to whom and to what we are attaching ourselves.

Any systematizing of theology is rather late on the church's scene. In the early church there were no catechisms, no theological tracts, no dictionaries of definitions. What did exist were homilies, apologies (arguments in defense of the church's beliefs), and creeds. Creeds were brief compositions of a state of a question of belief. In the early church there were many controversies. What beliefs many of us today take for granted had to be worked out in the early years of the church. Some people made errors (called "heresies") and led others astray. The way the church dealt with these differences of doctrinal understandings was to call church councils (sometimes quite local, sometimes regional, sometimes involving the larger church) to hammer out how they would interpret the gospel and the way of living to which it calls us.

The earliest creed we know is the baptismal creed which professes belief in a Triune God, in the Father's creating acts, in God's offer of salvation through Jesus Christ, and in the life given by the Spirit. The baptismal creed calls us to profess our acceptance of the holy, catholic (universal) church; the communion of saints; the forgiveness of sins; and eternal life. This baptismal creed — generally professed in the exchange of questions and "I do" responses — is captured in statement form in what has come to be called the Apostles' Creed. Contrary to some people's conclusion that this statement of belief was composed by the Apostles, this creed is so named because it dates to apostolic times — that is, the earliest time of the church.

As heresies crept up over the centuries of the church, other councils produced other creeds that captured in rather brief belief statements the church's official response to certain heretical teachings. Probably one of the most famous of the early council creeds is the Nicene Creed from the Council of Nicea (325 A.D.), which dealt with the Arian heresy, a controversy addressing the important issue of whether Jesus is divine (yes!). All these creeds are an important part of our church history. But in most cases the heresies or controversies that gave rise to councils and subsequently to creeds are not burning issues for us today. The one creed that remains fundamental is the baptismal creed, the Apostles' Creed. It summarizes for us the apostolic faith.

Since the Apostles' Creed is so closely linked to baptism, there is a distinct advantage to including this profession of apostolic faith in our Sunday services. First of all, it connects us with a two-millennia tradition of worshiping Christian communities. It also reminds us that we gather on Sunday — the Lord's Day, the day of resurrection — precisely because we have professed our belief in Jesus Christ, have declared our desire to follow him as disciples, and have chosen to surrender ourselves to this body of people who make visible the Body of Christ into which we are baptized. The creed publicly professed during Sunday worship connects each Sunday to our baptismal event and renews our commitment to live the gospel as Jesus calls us.

CONFESSION

Jesus' words are comforting: "Those who are well have no need of a physician, but those who are sick. Go and learn what this means, 'I desire mercy, not sacrifice.' For I have come to call not the righteous but sinners" (Matt. 9:12-13). Since the beginning of humanity we have rebelled against God. We have forsaken the wonderful and easy relationship God desires with us, captured so beautifully in this image from Genesis: "They heard the sound of the LORD God walking in the garden at the time of the evening breeze . . ." (Gen. 3:8). Such an intimate scene. In this case three is not a crowd. We can imagine God, Adam, and Eve strolling through Paradise in the coolness and relaxation of the evening. But rebellion-sin destroyed this kind of companionable and easy relationship.

Sin has less to do with individual acts and more to do with attitudes and relationships. When we love someone dearly, we strive not to hurt, we strive to be generous, we strive to please. When our love grows dim, then the striving grows weak. When we stop working to deepen our love relationships, the connections begin to break down, we grow less aware of when we hurt, and we think of ourselves first rather than of our beloved. We know we have a hard enough time keeping faithful to our human love relationships. How much more so are we challenged in our relationship with the God who is unseen: "Those who say, 'I love God,' and hate their brothers or sisters, are liars; for those who do not love a brother or sister whom they have seen, cannot love God whom they have not seen. The commandment we have from him is this: those who love God must love their brothers and sisters also" (1 John 4:20-21). Our love for God is concretely measured by our love for others. The strength of our relationships with others reflects the strength of our relationship with God.

The Our Father reflects this same parallel of relationship with God and others. We have all prayed hundreds of times the petition about forgiveness: "And forgive us our debts, as we also have forgiven our debtors" (Matt. 6:12). The Greek text suggests a different translation for "have forgiven" — "forgave," which is stronger than its English translation: it makes God's forgiving us *conditional* on our forgiving each other. The point here is not a chicken-and-egg situation about forgiveness, but that our relationships with God and each other are inextricably connected. Which is also to say that our prayer to and worship of God cannot be separate from our attitudes, behaviors, and dispositions with each other.

An element of confession during worship services is something of a reality check. Confession calls us less to examine our consciences for individual sinful acts (although sometimes that may be necessary) than to commit to renewed relationships with each other that give evidence of our desire for an ever-renewing and deepening relationship with God. In other words, confession is more about adhering to God than it is about dwelling on our alienation. Confession is less concerned with sinfulness and more directed to conversion of heart that makes room for love to well up anew. Confession is less about sinfulness and more about growing in holiness.

INTERCESSIONS

Spiritual leaders often tell us that the most common kind of prayer we utter is petition. We humans always have needs. We are constantly turning to God to make our life easier, to heal us or someone close to us of pain or illness, to help us face difficulties as they arise. "O God, help me find a job." "O God, heal my niece of cancer." "O God, bring our soldiers home unharmed." "O God, help our high school team win the tournament." "O God, help my children grow up to be good and successful." All these petitions are legitimate. However, sometimes our petitionary prayer can sound like all we are doing is waiting for God to do the work of making our life right.

Intercessory prayer during worship is valuable because it reminds us that God is not the One to clean up our messes and problems; rather, petition is really about asking God to give us the strength and help we need to face and overcome whatever it is we are struggling with. Prayer petitions have a built-in nudge that helps us see our needs anew. For example, many of us have had the experience of praying for healing. Would it not be nice if we could be the ones bringing our loved one to Jesus on a mat — even being willing to go to the effort of climbing to the roof, breaking a hole in it, and lowering our sick one right into Jesus' midst (Luke 5:18-26)? There, right before Jesus' nose, we ask for healing. "You are loving and good. You won't ignore him." How nice to have that kind of immediacy with Jesus, that kind of subtle persuasion to receive the healing we so desperately wish for our loved one!

Miracles do happen. We hear about them. They just do not happen as often as we might like and when we want them to happen and to whom. The point of petitionary prayer is not to convince God to do what we want, but to orient ourselves to what God wants for us. When we ask God for our needs, it is our own attitudes and needs that change. We may not get physical healing for our loved one for whom we have petitioned God, but if we reflect more deeply, we might discover more serenity, surrender, a deeper faith, peace.

Prayers are always answered. The invitation of intercessory prayer during worship is to recognize that we partner with God in making ourselves and our world better. Intercessory prayer also invites us, challenges us, and helps us to align our wills more perfectly with God's will: "Your will be done on earth as it is in heaven" (Matt. 6:10). Oh, how important is intercessory prayer!

BLESSINGS

Often the benediction or blessing at worship comes near the end of the service, when people's minds are already at the brunch buffet and their bodies are eager to head that way. The benediction or blessing is usually very brief, and so it is easy to miss the significance of this ritual element and what it can teach us for our own daily living.

A blessing assures us of God's favor. It declares the sure calling and promise for carrying forward the renewed relationship with God and others that has happened during worship (no matter how imperceptible the change may be). It is comforting to be sent forth from worship with this special touch from God, knowing that we do not leave God in the worship space but rather that God dwells within each of us to guide and protect us in all we do.

Blessing occurs in any number of scriptural passages. Blessing always accompanies the passing on of a birthright, for example.

Perhaps the most beloved blessing is the blessing God commanded through Moses that "Aaron and his sons" are to give:

The Lord bless you and keep you;
the Lord make his face to shine upon you,
    and be gracious to you;
the Lord lift up his countenance upon you,
    and give you peace. (Num. 6:24-26)

Not only does this blessing assure the people of Israel of God's care, but the images of "face" and "countenance" are scriptural language for God's presence. Thus blessings make us sacred (consecrate us) because God is at all times present to us. God does not withdraw from us, but sometimes we withdraw from God. Blessings, then, invite us to open ourselves to God's abiding presence, to avail ourselves of God's sure help, to bask in God's care. Our greatest blessing is God's own gift of divine Self to us.

Blessing others is not limited to priests or ordained ministers, however. There has been a long history in the Judeo-Christian tradition of parents blessing children. One consequence of a deeper reflection on blessing as an element of worship is that it might give parents a language for blessing their children and might encourage them to make this a regular practice in the home. Parents might bless the little ones before they go to sleep at night, and the older children before they leave for school or head off to college or take the car out alone for the first time.

Blessings are not talismans; they are not magic. They are a worship element that connects us with God and each other. When blessings are given outside of a formal worship service, they are, nonetheless, a kind of worship. Who would consider that saying *Gesundheit* or "God bless you" when a person sneezes is actually an act of worship? Blessings are always a way to express a desire for goodness for the other. God's blessings are varied and rich. To bless another is to partner with God in showering this abundance of goodness on those we love and care for.

MISSION

As faithful as some people are to communal worship — especially the Sunday service — it is very easy to think only in terms of fulfilling one's allegiance or obligation to God by going to church and then forgetting about it. Even our language leaves something to be desired: we "go to" church. While, yes, "church" is a place to which we go (we need someplace to congregate), church is much more than a place. It is a meeting house, a rendezvous for encounter — with both God and each other. There ought to be nothing in a full understanding of worship about our fulfilling an obligation, then moving on with our lives as if worship and life have no connection whatsoever. Worship is connected with *mission* — with being sent to continue Jesus' saving ministry. Worship does have an obligation. But it is not simply to get to church services. Our obligation is primarily fulfilled not within the space of the service, but beyond the service and by how we live the gospel in our daily lives.

Some worship services have a formal, clear element of dismissal — of being sent forth to do God's work. This aspect of the relationship of worship and life, worship and caring for others is so important that we will pursue it extensively in the last chapter. Let it be enough here to mention it as a specific element of worship of which to be aware.

SILENCE

Probably the most absent element in worship for all too many congregations is silence. It is a truism to the point of being a cliché:

we do not live in a very quiet society, let alone a silent one. Noise, busyness, multitasking, deadlines, stress, and pressures all come crashing down on us. We often handle them by just taking on more activities, by turning up volumes on TVs and stereos, by having ear buds hammer away at us all day long. We are so used to sound and striving that when and if we ever stop, we are jittery, uncomfortable, ill at ease.

Silence is an essential element of worship because it stops time for us. It is a space to internalize and appropriate the movement of God during the worship. Too often worship is fast-paced, completely filled with sound, and goal-oriented. Adding silences to worship enables us to balance the pace and sound, to experience a rhythm between doing and resting, to open up a time and a space for us to catch up with ourselves so God can catch up with us.

Silence during worship is a beckon to Sabbath rest (Gen. 2:2). In spite of the clear commandment to rest (Exod. 20:8-11; Lev. 23:3; Deut. 5:12-15) one day a week, we hardly do that. Sunday seems to be the day when we do everything we have not accomplished the previous week so that we can start Monday with a clean slate. So we clean and shop and repair things and . . . and . . . and. . . . When we introduce silence during worship — not as an empty time of doing nothing and waiting for the next thing to begin, but as a time out of time filled with meaning — we are reminding ourselves that we are not in charge of our world or even of our own lives.

When God rested on the seventh day of creation, it was a time for God to revel in what had been created, a time to celebrate that something came out of nothing, out of chaos, out of a void (Gen. 1:1-2). It was a time to celebrate "very good" (Gen. 1:31). The one activity God did on the seventh day of divine rest was to bless and hallow the seventh day (Gen. 2:3). This day is set apart to appreciate what we are freely given. This day is hallowed because there is nothing more for God to accomplish other than relishing all that was done on the other six days.

The Christian Sunday is not a Jewish Sabbath. Sunday has a very unique meaning. It was on the first day of the week that Jesus was raised from the dead (John 20:1), that day when the whole meaning of Jesus' incarnation, life, ministry, suffering, and death became clear: "The Lord has risen indeed" (Luke 24:34). This is the day of new life. This is the day of hope fulfilled. This is the day when death is vanquished. This is the day when the righteous are vindicated. This is the day when Christians are forbidden to fast or kneel or be sad because this is the day when the risen Christ is present to bring us the Spirit and peace (John 20:21-22).

All of Sunday and what it means is a blessing. All of Sunday calls us to be silent in the face of a God who gives us life and salvation. All of Sunday reminds us that whoever we are and whatever we have is a gift from God. Sunday calls us to cease our productive activity and rest in the Lord. It calls us to remember that we are, indeed, wholly dependent upon God for our life and sustenance. Work focuses us on ourselves and what we can accomplish. Silence and rest focus us on God and what God desires for us and graciously, freely gives us: new life in the Spirit. If we never take silent moments, if we never rest, if we never take a full day just to celebrate God's blessings and goodness to us, then we miss an important aspect of the meaning of worship: that God gives us more than we could ever give God.

Moments of silence introduced at key transitional or significant moments during worship can serve as a conditioning for the kind of silence and rest that ought to characterize every Sunday. Silence during worship is the beginning point for Sunday rest. The silence and rest of worship is a "mini" Sabbath when we unite ourselves with the God who is so pleased with the goodness of creation. Sunday silence and rest — during worship and during the whole day — call us to be good stewards of this earth. They call us to a simpler life where goods are not at the center. They call us to take time to simply *be* with family and friends, building the kind of strong and pleasing relationships that lead us to a stronger and ever more pleasing relationship with God.

....

Reflecting Pause

The "forgotten" element of liturgy for which our congregation
   most longs is ... We feel fulfilled when ...
We pray best as a congregation when ... We find it most uncom-
   fortable to pray when ... We can't pray when ...
We are drawn to confession when ... We experience God's for-
   giveness when ... We experience others' forgiveness when ...
We forgive when ...
We run from silence in our daily living when ...
As a congregation, we run from silence during our worship ser-
   vices when ...
We crave silence when ...
About silence in daily life, we need to ...

....

So What, Really, Is Worship?

After all these pages of reflecting on so many aspects of what worship is, are we any closer to saying what, really, worship is? Perhaps a better way to put the question is whether we have grown in our appreciation for worship, grown in awe at the great privilege worship is, grown in our longing to renew and discover ever anew how God desires to be present to us. We have drawn on experience to discover aspects of worship — our own experience, the experience of grant applicants gleaned from the data from grant proposals. All this experience suggests to us that worship is greening in our midst. Among so many of us there is a great desire to learn how to worship better, to make worship the center of our lives, to grow in our relationship with God that is so very life-giving.

In the next chapters we will uncover other aspects of worship. So, we are not really ready yet to respond adequately to our question about the meaning of worship. Perhaps at this point we simply join ourselves to the heavenly hosts before the Lamb, where "there was silence in heaven for about half an hour" (Rev. 8:1).

CHAPTER 2

God's Word: A Primer on Worship?

Almighty God, your Word is cast
Like seed into the ground;
Now let the dew of heav'n descend
And righteous fruits abound.

John Cawood, "Almighty God, Your Word Is Cast," verse 1

GOD'S DIVINELY INSPIRED word as recorded in the Hebrew and Christian Scriptures has been an integral part of worship throughout the long history of the Judeo-Christian tradition. God's word has guided us in constructing our private and communal prayer and our rhythm of festivals and seasons. It also has been an invariable element in our actual worship services. God's word is the basis for the synagogue service. There it is read, studied, meditated on, and prayed. God's word is the ground for Christian worship. There it is proclaimed, broken open, and prayed. God's word forms the basis for some of our most beloved prayers — for example, the Our Father (Matt. 6:9-13; Luke 11:2-4), the *Magnificat* (Luke 1:46-55; prayed at evening prayer in some traditions), the *Benedictus* (Luke 1:68-79; prayed at morning prayer in some traditions), and the *Nunc Dimittus* (Luke 2:29-32; prayed at night prayer in some traditions).

God's word is the inspiration for blessing (Num. 6:24-26; Deut. 33:2-29) and praise (Deut. 32:1-3). God's word is the seed of confession (Ps. 51; Job 42:2-6) and lament (Job 23:2-17). God's word gives us language for thanksgiving (Isa. 12:1-6) and adoration (Isa. 6:3).

Scripture was referenced surprisingly few times when grant applicants grappled with the question of worship. Two of the most common references were John 4:24 and Psalm 100 (both examined at length below). Other references included the following passages, all from the New Testament:

> You shall love the Lord your God with all your heart, and with all your soul, and with all your strength, and with all your mind; and your neighbor as yourself. (Luke 10:27)

> I appeal to you therefore, brothers and sisters, by the mercies of God, to present your bodies as a living sacrifice, holy and acceptable to God, which is your spiritual worship. Do not be conformed to this world, but be transformed by the renewing of your minds, so that you may discern what is the will of God — what is good and acceptable and perfect. (Rom. 12:1-2)

> Let the word of Christ dwell in you richly; teach and admonish one another in all wisdom; and with gratitude in your hearts sing psalms, hymns, and spiritual songs to God. And whatever you do, in word or deed, do everything in the name of the Lord Jesus, giving thanks to God the Father through him. (Col. 3:16-17)

> And the four living creatures, each of them with six wings, are full of eyes all around and inside. Day and night without ceasing they sing,
> "Holy, holy, holy,

> the Lord God the Almighty,
>   who was and is and is to come."

And whenever the living creatures give glory and honor and thanks to the one who is seated on the throne, who lives forever and ever, the twenty-four elders fall before the one who is seated on the throne and worship the one who lives forever and ever; they cast their crowns before the throne, singing,
>   "You are worthy, our Lord and God,
>   to receive glory and honor and power,
>   for you created all things,
>   and by your will they existed
>   and were created." (Rev. 4:8-11)

Scripture includes many fragments of hymns or songs, which also give us an insight into a language for worship and the meaning of worship. Before the Israelites crossed over into the Promised Land, Moses sang a lengthy song that not only gave God praise but also instructed the people in God's ways (Deut. 32:1-43). And Miriam danced (Exod. 15:20)! When Hannah brings the newborn Samuel to the Temple to offer him to God, she prays a hymn which parallels Mary's *Magnificat* at the annunciation of Jesus (1 Sam. 2:1-10; see Luke 1:46-55). Other Old Testament hymns or songs or canticles include Exodus 15:1-18; 15:21; 1 Chronicles 29:10-13; Tobit 13:1-17; Judith 16:1-17; Sirach 36:1-22; Isaiah 12:1-6; 26:1-21; 42:10-25; Daniel 3:52-90. The New Testament also abounds with hymns, songs, and canticles. Over and above the three Gospel canticles already mentioned, consider Philippians 2:5-11; Colossians 1:15-20; Revelation 4:11; 5:9-14; 11:17-18; 12:10-12; 15:3-4; 16:5-7; 19:1-8.

The most extensive collection of prayers in all of Scripture, of course, is the book of Psalms. These 150 song-prayers capture the whole gamut of human postures before God: praise, adoration, thanksgiving, petition, confession, lament, homage, judgment, justice — and the list could go on. The psalms also express a whole range of human emotions: love, forgiveness, anger, vengeance, compassion, longing, trust, joy, need, confidence, patience, intimacy, anguish — and more could be mentioned. There are psalms begging for help, expressing confidence in God as deliverer, stating confidence in God's presence, begging for blessings, seeking protection, praying for healing. Every one of the 150 psalms captures something of the essence of our relationship with the Divine One as well as with each other. Is it any wonder that the psalms form the backbone of both Jewish and Christian prayer?

When we pray the psalms alone or use psalms together in worship, we have in our hearts and on our lips the very words Jesus himself prayed. St. Joseph must have been a good foster father and teacher of Jesus, for we catch glimpses in the Gospels of Jesus having committed these ancient words to memory and heart. On the cross, in his most desolate moment, a psalm is on his lips, giving him words to express the depth of his pain and suffering: "My God, my God, why have you forsaken me?" (Ps. 22:1; Matt. 27:46; Mark 15:34). Often Jesus' language of teaching reflects the language of the psalms. Consider these examples:

- Blessed are the pure in heart. . . . (Matt. 5:8) // Who shall ascend the hill of the LORD? And who shall stand in his holy place? Those who have clean hands and pure hearts. . . . (Ps. 24:3-4)
- Look at the birds of the air; they neither sow nor reap nor gather into barns, and yet your heavenly Father feeds them. (Matt. 6:26) // The eyes of all look to you, and you give them their food in due season. (Ps. 145:15) // He gives to the animals their food, and to the young ravens when they cry. (Ps. 147:9)

- And they went and woke him up, saying, "Lord, save us! We are perishing!" And he said to them, "Why are you afraid, you of little faith?" Then he got up and rebuked the winds and the sea; and there was dead calm. (Matt. 8:25-26) // . . . he made the storm be still, and the waves of the sea were hushed. (Ps. 107:29)
- I will open my mouth to speak in parables. . . . (Matt. 13:35) // I will open my mouth in a parable. . . . (Ps. 78:2)
- . . . he will repay everyone for what has been done. (Matt. 16:27) // For you repay all according to their work. (Ps. 62:12)
- Hosanna to the Son of David! Blessed is the one who comes in the name of the Lord! Hosanna in the highest heaven! (Matt. 21:9; also, Matt. 23:39) // Blessed is the one who comes in the name of the LORD! (Ps. 118:26)
- Jesus said to them, "Have you never read in the scriptures: 'The stone that the builders rejected has become the cornerstone; this was the Lord's doing, and it is amazing in our eyes'? . . ." (Matt. 21:42) // The stone that the builders rejected has become the cornerstone. This is the LORD's doing; it is marvelous in our eyes. (Ps. 118:22-23)
- He said to them, "How is it then that David by the Spirit calls him Lord, saying, 'The Lord said to my Lord, "Sit at my right hand, until I put your enemies under your feet"'? . . ." (Matt. 22:43-44) // The LORD says to my lord, "Sit at my right hand until I make your enemies your footstool." (Ps. 110:1)

Would that our own speech utterances and prayers would draw so familiarly on Sacred Scripture! Would that the psalms were so written in our hearts that in times of joy and trouble their words well up as our own words!

....

Reflecting Pause

To our congregation, God's inspired word means . . .
We are most drawn to use God's inspired word in our personal
    prayer when . . .
We are most drawn to use God's inspired word in our congrega-
    tion's services when . . .
When God's word is proclaimed during worship, our response is
    usually . . .
What draws us regularly to ponder God's word in Sacred Scrip-
    ture is . . .

....

The Ancient Code: Worship Draws Us
into God's Holiness, God's Very Life

We can learn much about worship from many books of the Bible.
In a few cases specific liturgies are spelled out in quite some detail. The best known of these is probably the institution of the first
Passover, celebrated on the eve before the tenth plague destroyed
the firstborn of all Egypt (Exod. 12:1-28). This divinely ordained
ritual defines Israel as a people who were brought by God from
slavery to freedom. Its annual celebration each spring enacts Israel's "passing over" from slavery to freedom, from sin to grace,
from no people to God's chosen people. This is Israel's "paschal"
event. This is Israel's founding evening.

Another paschal event is foretold at a liturgy described in the
New Testament. Luke's account of the Lord's Supper has Jesus describing to his apostles that "This cup that is poured out for you
is the new covenant in my blood" (Luke 22:20). The blood of the

slain lamb smeared on the doorposts of the houses of the Israelites to protect them from the slayer's hand becomes the blood of the Lamb poured out that leads his faithful followers through death to new life. Both Matthew and Mark place this Lamb's blood poured out within an eschatological (pertaining to the fulfillment of the end times) context: "Truly I tell you, I will never again drink of the fruit of the vine until that day when I drink it new in the kingdom of God" (Mark 14:25; cf. Matt. 26:29).

Perhaps no richer insight into worship is offered than that found in the so-called holiness code of the book of Leviticus (chaps. 17–26). Over and over again, Leviticus reiterates that God is holy: "For I am the LORD your God . . . be holy, for I am holy" (Lev. 11:44-45). Holiness is of the essence of God; it is who God is. We cannot see God's holiness, but we do see and experience its manifestation: glory. Creation abounds in manifestations of God's holiness: the glorious color of a sunrise or sunset; the glorious pounding of the oceans' waves; the glorious majesty of the great Sequoias; the glorious expanse of the Arctic ice cap; the glorious beauty of a newborn baby; the glorious radiance of a graduate; the glorious peace of grandparents. God created all things, and they are very good. God's very countenance is traced in all creation. At moments of coming face to face with God's glory, we cannot help but have our hearts well up in wonder and gratitude and be moved to worship with awe.

God's glory (presence) requires of us immediate response. When Moses encounters the burning bush and approaches it out of curiosity, God addresses him with this command: ". . . Remove the sandals from your feet, for the place on which you are standing is holy ground" (Exod. 3:5). Taking off one's shoes is an Eastern custom of respect. Through this command God is announcing to Moses that one greater than he is present. But another allegorical interpretation may be suggested by this passage. When Moses takes off his sandals, he is removing anything that comes between his body and the "holy ground." It can be a gesture interpreted as coming closer to the Holy One, removing any obstacle that gets in the way of being present to divine Presence.

Unmediated face-to-face contact with the Holy One reminds us of the distance between our imperfect selves and the all-holy God. When Isaiah has his vision of "the Lord sitting on a throne, high and lofty" (Isa. 6:1) and hears the winged Seraphs call to one another, "Holy, holy, holy is the LORD of hosts; the whole earth is full of his glory" (Isa. 6:3), he is fearful for his very life: "Woe is me! I am lost, for I am a man of unclean lips, and I live among a people of unclean lips; yet my eyes have seen the King, the LORD of hosts!" (Isa. 6:5). Isaiah is cleansed with a burning coal touched to his mouth and responds to the LORD's call with renewed courage and eagerness: "Here am I; send me!" (Isa. 6:8). It is comforting to know that God does not expect us to be perfect, either in order to worship God or to answer the divine call to serve. All God asks is an eager heart: "Here am I; send me!"

Because God is holy, God's people are holy: "Speak to all the congregation of the people of Israel and say to them: You shall be holy, for I the LORD your God am holy" (Lev. 19:2). Over and over again in the holiness code of Leviticus, God affirms that we are holy. For example, "Consecrate yourselves therefore, and be holy; for I am the LORD your God" (Lev. 20:7). And "You shall be holy to me; for I the LORD am holy, and I have separated you from the other peoples to be mine" (Lev. 20:26). One purpose of worship is to celebrate not only God's holiness, but our own. Notice what these passages are saying, however. We are holy not because of what we do, but because God chooses to relate to us and share with us divine life. It is this sharing in God's life that makes us holy. However, when we recognize this great gift of sharing in God's very being (in theology this has traditionally been called "grace"), our response is to desire to live the life that God has given us. Thus, worship does have its ethical demands (addressed more extensively in Chapter 4). Leviticus spells out those ethical demands. The first example comes from Leviticus 18:2-5: ". . . I am the LORD your God. You shall not do as they do in the land of Canaan, to which I am bringing you. You shall not follow their statutes. My ordinances you shall observe and my statutes you shall keep, following them . . . by doing so one shall live: I am the LORD." The second example comes from Leviticus 22:31: "Thus you shall keep my commandments, and observe them: I am the LORD. You shall not profane my holy name, that I may be sanctified among the people of Israel: I am the LORD; I sanctify you, I who brought you out of the land of Egypt to be your God: I am the LORD." Notice the context of the command to keep God's laws: it is not law for law's sake; rather, we keep God's commandments because God leads us to freedom and shares divine life with us. Keeping God's laws is not merely an ethical injunction; keeping God's laws is a concrete expression of our covenantal relationship with God, of our openness to the life God offers us.

The holiness code of Leviticus includes cultic laws (that is, laws having to do with worship): "They shall be holy to their God, and not profane the name of their God; for they offer the LORD's offerings by fire, the food of their God; therefore they shall be holy" (Lev. 21:6). Leviticus also lays out a cycle of annual feasts: "Speak to the people of Israel and say to them: These are the appointed festivals of the LORD that you shall proclaim as holy convocations, my appointed festivals" (Lev. 23:2). Worship's holy actions and the year's holy festivals all flow from the all-holy God and the divine life in which God invites us to participate. Worship, then, captures God's glory and reveals a trace of God's divine presence. The encounter with God we seek during worship draws us deeper into God's very essence, God's very being, God's very holiness. Worship draws us deeper into who we are and are becoming: the beloved of God, God's very own people.

There is no equivalent book in the New Testament that gives us the same breadth of a picture of worship, either in terms of statutes and laws or in terms of an annual cycle of festivals. Still, we do learn more from other New Testament books. Matthew gives us the Great Commission: "Go therefore and make disciples of all nations, baptizing them in the name of the Father and of the Son and of the Holy Spirit" (Matt. 28:19). Concerning the Lord's Supper, Jesus gives us this command that we read in Luke: "Do this in remembrance of me" (Luke 22:19). Paul instructs the Corinthians about proper attitudes and behaviors at the celebration of the Lord's Supper (1 Cor. 11:17-34), and gives us a clear sense of what it is we are really celebrating: "For as often as you eat this bread and drink this cup, you proclaim the Lord's death until he comes" (1 Cor. 11:26). He also makes the ethical demands of the communal celebration of the Lord's Supper quite clear: "Whoever, therefore, eats the bread or drinks the cup of the Lord in an unworthy manner will be answerable for the body and blood of the Lord. . . . For all who eat and drink without discerning the body, eat and drink judgment against themselves. . . . If you are hungry, eat at home, so that when you come together, it will not be for your condemnation" (1 Cor. 11:27, 29, 34).

Hidden in Paul's condemnation of the Supper practices of the Corinthian Christian community is a theme about liturgy that is picked up in the early Christian writers and becomes quite prominent. As liturgy, participation in the Lord's Supper transforms us into being more perfect members of the Body of Christ. Since at the Lord's Supper we proclaim Jesus' death and resurrection, our participation in that celebration is a participation in Jesus' saving events. As one member of the Body is transformed, so is the whole Body transformed. If one member is not given over to the good of the whole Body, then the whole Body suffers. The ethical import the Lord's Supper has at stake is nothing less than the health of the Body. (The Hebrew root for the word "salvation" means "health, well-being, wholeness.")

It was left to the early church to develop an annual cycle of festivals that make present the broad scope of Jesus' life and saving minis-try. For at least the first century of the church's existence, the weekly gathering for the breaking of the bread was the defining moment for the Christian communities. Gradually there developed a felt need to have an annual celebration of the Lord's death and resurrection in the springtime (Northern hemisphere) when those historical events took place. By the middle of the second century, we have clear evidence of this annual celebration of the Easter events. But it was not until the beginning of the fourth century, with the Peace of Constantine (313 A.D., Edict of Milan), that Christians could freely and openly prac-tice their Christian faith. At this time other festivals (e.g., Christmas, Epiphany, Ascension, Pentecost) began to develop and be celebrated.

Paralleling the development of the seasons of the church year that celebrate the key events in the life and ministry of Jesus, there also developed annual commemorations of holy people whom the early church wished to keep before their communities as witnesses to holy lives. From earliest times, martyrs (from the Greek word meaning "witness") have been held in high esteem by Christians because the martyrs so totally conformed their lives to Christ's life that they even willingly went to their death rather than deny their allegiance to Christ. Like Jesus, the martyrs' faithful deaths were celebrated as occasions for their being raised to new, risen, and eternal life. Like Jesus, they passed over from death to life. So it be-came customary to build Christian churches over the burial places of martyrs, thus making a strong connection among martyrdom, the Lord's Supper, and resurrection. Annually the local communi-ties would celebrate on the anniversary of their local martyr's death (the martyr's entrance into risen life) the Lord's Supper.

When the age of martyrdom essentially concluded with the Peace of Constantine, the church began to hold up other men and women as holy ones, as saints to be emulated. These holy people were called "confessors" because they "confessed" their belief and commitment to Christ by the way they lived, often heroically. Eventually these saints also found their place on the church's annual calendar of celebrations. We remember them because they show us what holy lives look like, what conforming to Christ in everyday living is, what it means to surrender oneself totally to Christ and remain faithful throughout one's life to baptismal commitment. We honor John the Baptist, Mary, Joseph, martyrs, confessors, and other good people because they help us to live like Jesus lived and lead us to God. We do not worship them, but we honor them for their goodness and holiness.

There is much in the ancient code of the Sacred Scriptures that points us in the direction of fruitful worship. At the same time, both worship and the church's calendar have undergone many changes throughout the two millennia of Christian practice and worship. Worship is not a stagnant ceremony, but a living community of men and women, children and youth who turn themselves toward God through uniting themselves with Christ in his own turning toward his Father in heaven.

....

Reflecting Pause

The Scripture passage about worship that has most struck us is
    ... because ...
As a congregation, we experience a passing over from slavery to
    freedom, from death to life, when ...
To us, holiness means ... We believe ourselves to be holy when ...
Holiness gives our congregation deeper insight about worship in
    that ...
The elements of worship that we might need to reconsider in
    order to more clearly connect holiness and worship are ...

....

The Psalm-Songs: Ancient Prayers Teach Us about Worship

We spoke above about the psalms as Jesus' prayer and the church's prayer. The psalms are also a rich source for coming to a deeper understanding of worship. A close reading of them uncovers elements, structures, and reasons for worship. Each psalm can reveal something about us, God, our relationships, and how this might be expressed in worship. It is not possible to examine each psalm here from a worship perspective, so I have chosen a few prime examples for close reading to move us forward in our understanding of what worship is.

ASCENDENCY PSALMS: ELEMENTS OF WORSHIP

Some praise psalms are "ascendency" psalms, a title given to a group of psalms that were most likely used as the people went up to worship. "Up" is the operative term here, and its meaning in the context of the ascendency psalms is dependent on an understanding of how ancient Israel understood the structure of their world.

The Hebrew world was considered to be flat, with a region above the earth (the heavens) and a region below the earth (the underworld or Hades). God dwelt above the earth, in the heavens, and so if one wanted to be in communion with God, the idea was to go up. Moses went up Mount Sinai to talk with God and receive the Ten Commandments (Exod. 19, 20). Elijah met God up on Mount Horeb in the "sound of sheer silence" (1 Kings 19:11-12). The Temple in Jerusalem was built up on a hill. Jesus' favorite place for prayer was up on the Mount of Olives. One of the most beautiful ascendency psalms is Psalm 24, where "up" imagery occurs multiple times: "Who shall ascend [go up] the hill of the LORD?" (v. 3a); "Lift up your heads, O gates! and be lifted up, O ancient doors!" (v. 7a, b; this verse is repeated at v. 9ab).

Although most of our contemporary worship spaces are not built on mountain tops, going *up* is an apt metaphor for a disposition we might have as we come to worship. Our communal worship services are an invitation to raise ourselves up out of the ordinary daily happenings and concerns, and surrender ourselves to a most uplifting time-out-of-time. We also might think of gathering for communal worship as a going "up," for we leave our homes or apartments and go toward a common worship space.

It is natural to expect that psalms sung on pilgrimage to the temple or upon entering the temple would be characterized by praise (and thanksgiving). There are many praise psalms in the book of Psalms, and analyzing them gives us a broad understanding of our relationship with God — how good God has been to us, how God helps us, why we are in covenantal relationship with God. One praise psalm in particular summarizes quite nicely key elements of worship. Psalm 100 is a remarkable psalm in that it tells us so much *about* worship at the same time that praying the psalm is worship in itself. This is a fairly short psalm, with only five verses (and from it comes the title for this book):

1   Make a joyful noise to the LORD, all the earth.
2   Worship the LORD with gladness;
    come into his presence with singing.

3   Know that the LORD is God.
    It is he that made us, and we are his;
    we are his people, and the sheep of his pasture.

4   Enter his gates with thanksgiving,
    and his courts with praise.
    Give thanks to him, bless his name.

5   For the LORD is good;
     his steadfast love endures forever,
     and his faithfulness to all generations. (Ps. 100)

Four strophes (psalm language for "stanza") make up this psalm,
and they can be neatly divided in half, with each half forming a
poem in itself. The first strophe tells us how we approach the worship of God: with joy and gladness and song. This does not suggest
that we leave our pain and difficulties at the door of the worship
space. It does mean that during worship, when we consciously
place ourselves in God's presence, for those brief moments we
can be free of our worries and troubles and rejoice that God is our
creator and that we belong to God, that God is with us during our
daily living and lifts us up out of our lowly human condition. Then
in the second strophe we see why we lift our hearts in praise. Given
God's unfailing faithfulness in the past, we are confident that God
is faithful now because we are the work of God's creative hand
and God has chosen us to be God's people. Such dignity God has
bestowed on God's beloved!

The first half of Psalm 100, then, speaks to us of worship as

- a joyful coming into God's presence (vv. 1-2),
- an invitation for everyone to worship (v. 1b),
- a recognition that God is God and we are not God (v. 3a),
- an acknowledgment of God as creator (v. 3b), and
- a proclamation that we are God's people for whom God cares
  (v. 3c).

The last two strophes shift from praise to thanksgiving, and if the
first two strophes give us the reason for our praise, so do the last
two give us the reason for thanksgiving. The psalm acknowledges
that God is good, that God unfailingly loves us (with a mercy-love

that includes tenderness, compassion, forgiveness, and care) and all the generations after us. God is faithful, and because of that unwavering fidelity we know that we are never alone, that our human life can never defeat us, that God is always with us. These two strophes suggest that worship is

- coming to God with thankful hearts because we can enumerate all that God does for us (v. 4),
- proclaiming God's goodness to us (v. 5a),
- acknowledging God's enduring acts of love (v. 5b), and
- recognizing that our relationship with God extends forever (v. 5c).

Psalm 100 caps a series of praise psalms, beginning with Psalm 95's call to worship.

Like Psalm 100, Psalm 95 begins by beckoning us to "sing to the LORD . . . [and] make a joyful noise" to God. It calls forth reverence from us (v. 6) and echoes the words of Psalm 100, affirming that we are God's people (v. 7). Psalm 95 urges us to hear and heed God's voice (v. 7b) and not to be stubborn about what God asks of us (vv. 8-9). All the psalms in this series begin with an invitation to sing a joyful song to the LORD. The next psalm, Psalm 96, bids us to proclaim God's mighty deeds (v. 3), bids us to attribute to God what is due the divine Being (vv. 7-8a), admonishes us to bring God an offering (v. 8b), reminds us that God judges with fairness (vv. 10c and 13c), and concludes with several verses announcing that all the heavens and earth are to be joyful at God's coming. Psalm 97 extols God for divine justice (vv. 2b and 6), for divine enemies being destroyed (v. 3), for God guarding and rescuing us from evil (v. 10); it also admonishes us to rejoice and give thanks for such a God. Psalm 98 extols God as victorious (vv. 1b, 2a, 3c) and invites us to be joyful at the presence of God

(vv. 4-9a), who comes with righteous judgment (vv. 9b, c). Psalm 99 sings praises for God's holiness (v. 5b), for God's speaking to us (v. 7), for God's forgiveness (v. 8b), and ends by once again extolling God's holiness (v. 9c).

These praise psalms (and others in the book of Psalms) clearly show that our worship is oriented to God, that our worship is a response to God's marvelous deeds on our behalf, that we bow before God in worship because God is our Creator, Redeemer, and Sanctifier. Most important in all of this is that the psalms model for us how we are constantly to remember God's mighty deeds on our behalf. God's mighty deeds are the motivation for our worship-response. It is these mighty deeds that invite us to fidelity because God is faithful, that urge us to worship because God is manifestly deserving of our awe and reverence, that bring forth from us praise and thanksgiving because God has dealt with us not as enemies but as a beloved people called to be God's own. Even when we stray from God's friendship, God still loves us and calls us into divine presence with mercy and love.

....

Reflecting Pause

As a congregation, we feel the urge to go "up" to God when . . .
We praise God for . . . This leads to thanksgiving when . . .
As a congregation, we experience that we are God's own when . . .
We feel alienated from God when . . .
God has been good to us in these ways . . .
When we think together about moments in our public worship,
    we are drawn to God in . . .

....

69

Psalms of Lament: A Structure of Worship

The most common genre of psalm in the book of Psalms is the lament, with almost half the psalms being either an individual or a communal lament. What we can learn from these psalms is that the psalmist is not complaining just for complaining's sake; the lament brings about a transformation in the individual or community. In this sense the laments have a structure that very much parallels the structure of worship. All lament psalms do not follow exactly the same structural order or include invariable elements. But there is a flow to the laments that teach us something about how we might structure our worship. Psalm 13 (an individual lament) is a good example of the flow of a lament. Let us do a close reading of this psalm:

1   How long, O LORD?
Will you forget me forever?
How long will you hide your face from me?

2   How long must I bear pain in my soul,
and have sorrow in my heart all day long?
How long shall my enemy be exalted over me?

3   Consider and answer me,
O LORD my God!
Give light to my eyes, or I will sleep the sleep of death,

4   and my enemy will say, "I have prevailed";
my foes will rejoice because I am shaken.

5   But I trusted in your steadfast love;
my heart shall rejoice in your salvation.

6   I will sing to the LORD,
because he has dealt bountifully with me.

The psalm begins with an address to God in the form of questions (vv. 1-2), and in the very invocation the lament is already expressed. The psalmist is in anguish because God seems to have forgotten (v. 1a) and hidden (v. 1b) from him or her. The psalmist's pain is focused on God's seeming absence, but also on the fact that he or she has lost face — enemies are gloating that the psalmist's God is not present to comfort and guard (vv. 2c and 4). Losing face here is more than an embarrassment: it is a life-threatening matter of being cut off from God's protection, help, life. This heart-wrenching lament is followed by the psalmist's plea for help (v. 3): the plea is for "light to my eyes." Light might be an image referring to seeing God, once again experiencing God's nearness that the psalmist perceives to have been lost. Then the psalmist remembers God's faithfulness in never withholding love and salvation (v. 5). All will be well, and so the psalmist breaks forth in praise-song (v. 6). Some lament psalms add another element after coming to praise — that is, a resolve to be faithful to God. A very clear example of a lament concluding with a resolve is Psalm 31, which ends this way: "Love the LORD, all you his saints. . . . Be strong, and let your heart take courage, all you who wait for the LORD" (vv. 23a, 24).

The chart on the next page indicates six elements of lament (not present in every lament psalm and not always in this order), and their parallels with elements of a worship service.

In a typical Sunday service, some of the elements might not be arranged quite in this order. For example, in many cases it makes sense that the intercessions or prayer of the day would follow the proclamation of God's word and preaching, which give a context for our prayers. If the worship service is not a liturgy of the Lord's Supper, then obviously the Great Thanksgiving would not be present. But most worship services will have some kind of litany or prayer praising and thanking God for all God's blessings, some-

Element of Lament	Element of Worship
Invocation	Greeting and opening prayer
Complaint	Confession
Plea for help	Intercession
Remembering God's deeds	Proclaiming God's word
Praise of God and thanksgiving	Litany of praise or a Great Thanksgiving
Resolve to be faithful	Dismissal to live as disciples

times specific to happenings in the congregants' lives during the previous week.

Obviously, there are other elements that are traditionally incorporated into worship. Hymns, songs, antiphons, and canticles are surely important ones. The psalms themselves are songs, so the laments are songs as well. The Song of Songs is an entire book of the Bible devoted to the singing of an extended love ode between the Beloved and the beloved. Dance might be an important element of worship. For example, Miriam and other women danced and sang to the Lord (Exod. 15:20-21), and David danced before the Lord when the Ark of the Covenant was brought up to Jerusalem (2 Sam. 6:14, 21). Also, in the very last psalm we are invited to praise God with dance (Ps. 150:4a), and in that well-sung passage from the book of Ecclesiastes we are reminded that there is "a time to dance" (Eccles. 3:4b). Different elements of worship and how we structure them can be quite varied, limited only by our own imaginations and hearts.

The intent in teasing out the structure of laments is not to give an invariable structure to worship. But a study of laments does show us that our very human needs and concerns not only have a place in worship, but are proper to worship itself. God wants us to be ourselves as we come before the divine Majesty to surrender ourselves to God's loving presence. Laments show us that complaining about what is painful for us can lead us to transformation. The bridge between complaint and praise and thanksgiving is remembering God's mighty deeds for us, God's everlasting faithfulness, and God's unstinting love and compassion. These are what lead us to praise and thanksgiving. These are what encourage us to renew our own covenant with God, our own resolve to be faithful. These mighty deeds of God and God's loving relationship to us draw us into worship and bring our hearts to spill over in love and gratitude, praise and worship.

....

Reflecting Pause

At this point in our common life, our congregation's own psalm of
    lament is this:
The words in our lament that capture the elements of lament
    are . . .

....

THANKSGIVING PSALMS:
FOR WHAT DO WE GIVE THANKS?

Many of the laments end not only in praise, but also in thanksgiving. When the thanksgiving is extended, then the psalm itself might be classified as a thanksgiving psalm. A close reading of these psalms catalog for us a simple enough structure, often just twofold: a rehearsal of what God has done for the psalmist (a statement of God's mighty deeds) and then exaltation and thanksgiving for God's goodness. For example, Psalm 28:1-5 rehearses the psalmist's plea for help — specifically, to be delivered from the wicked and "workers of evil" who have "mischief in their hearts" (v. 3); then the psalm moves to praise and thanksgiving (vv. 6-9). Psalm 30 expresses the psalmist's account of being healed, and it must have been a grave situation because he or she then declares, "I will give thanks to you forever" (v. 12b). Psalm 92 begins right off with giving thanks, saying it is good to do so (v. 1a); the reason for the thankful heart is God's great works (v. 5), the destruction of the wicked (vv. 7b, 9), and the prosperity of the righteous (vv. 12-15). Psalm 107 also begins with explicit thanksgiving (v. 1a); the reason for thanksgiving is God's deliverance of those in distress (vv. 6b, 13b, 19b-20, 28b), God's steadfast love (vv. 8a, 15a, 21a, 31a, 43b), and God's wonderful works (vv. 8b, 21b, 22b, 24, 33-42). Notice the marvelous repetition in this psalm, with the three motifs of deliverance, divine love, and God's deeds constantly coming back in repetition. Repetition is a construct of Hebrew poetry which serves to add emphasis to what is being prayed. These three motifs could really capture all of God's relationship to God's people and summarize whatever other reasons for giving thanks we might have.

Psalm 111 gives thanks to God for the great divine works (vv. 1-2) and then describes those works in terms of divine righteousness (v. 3b); graciousness and mercy (v. 4b); provision of food (v. 5a); giving to God's people the nations' heritage (v. 6b); and God's faithfulness, justice, and trustworthiness (vv. 7, 8b). This psalm emphasizes the attributes of God more than the deeds God does (although attributes and deeds cannot really be separated). Psalm 116 thanks God (v. 17) for deliverance from distress and anguish (v. 3c) and great affliction (v. 10b). Psalm 138 twice gives thanks to God (vv. 1a, 2b), again for God's hearing the plea of the psalmist for help (v. 3), for God's paying attention to the lowly (v. 6a), and for preservation from enemies (v. 7b).

In all, no fewer than thirty-three psalms (over one-fifth of the collection) mention thanks or thanksgiving. Psalm 118 has five verses that explicitly mention giving God thanks (vv. 1a, 19b, 21a, 28a, 29a). What is structurally interesting in this psalm is that the refrain "his steadfast love endures forever" is repeated five times (vv. 1b, 2b, 3b, 4b, 29b), although not always coupled with a verse giving thanks. A similar pattern is found in Psalm 136: explicit mention of giving God thanks (four times: vv. 1a, 2a, 3a, 26a), with the phrase "his steadfast love endures forever" not only directly coupled with giving thanks (vv. 1b, 2b, 3b, 26b), but also occurring as a litany-like refrain for the whole middle section of the psalm, which recites God's work of creation and salvation (vv. 4-25).

These thanksgiving psalms not only enumerate for us all for which we give God thanks; they also remind us that the greatest act of thanksgiving is directed to the very being of God, who is everything for us. Any act of worship cannot help but include thanksgiving, not in some general, abstract way but in the concrete way of acknowledging who God is for us and all God has done and continues to do for us.

....

Reflecting Pause

Our congregation gives thanks for who God is for us when . . .
We are most likely to include an element of thanksgiving in our
    communal worship when . . .
We give thanks for what God has done for us when . . .
We give thanks for what God is doing for us when . . .
Our litany of thanks to God looks like this:

....

John 4:24: From Human Encounter
to Jesus as Messiah-Savior

As mentioned earlier, the Scripture passage that occurred most frequently in the grant proposals in response to the question about the meaning of worship was John 4:24: "God is spirit, and those who worship him must worship in spirit and truth." To appreciate this passage fully and for it to help us understand worship better, we must place it in the context of the entire gospel pericope (scriptural language for a passage, a story). The scene is Jesus' encounter with the Samaritan woman at the well (John 4:4-42). It is a story filled with trust, wonder, insight, revelation, confession, and evangelization. It is a story with many detours on its road from beginning to end.

Before we travel that road, let us set the scene. Jesus is journeying from Judea (in the south) to Galilee (in the north). The usual road is through Samaria, and "Jews do not share things in common with Samaritans" (v. 9b). The reason for this rift goes back to the Babylonian Captivity (587-38 B.C.), when the Temple was destroyed and Jews were deported to Babylon. Living in a foreign land, they could not worship their God as they had been accustomed to doing, especially by offering sacrifices. The Samaritans, on the other hand, were not involved in this deportation and could continue their customary worship on Mount Gerizim. Where to worship is the basis for the rift at the time when Jesus encounters the Samaritan woman, but it is not the real story of the story.

Jesus is tired and thirsty. So the road we travel during this pericope begins with an encounter between Jesus and the woman on a level of very human need: Jesus' thirst for just plain old water from the well. It ends with the woman being a disciple-witness to Jesus, the true Messiah. The real insight of the pericope is that once one encounters Jesus, neither Mount Gerizim nor the Temple in Jerusalem is the true place to worship God. When Jesus tells the woman "I am" in response to her comments about the expectation of the Messiah (v. 26a), he is announcing, in effect, that he himself is the place of worship. This "I am" parallels Jesus' self-revelation in the Garden (in John's Gospel account) when Judas and the soldiers come looking for him to arrest him and take him to his trial. Jesus takes command of the scene by asking who the soldiers want; they answer "Jesus of Nazareth" (John 18:5), and Jesus responds (twice) with "I am" (vv. 5a, 8a). This "I am" is the same divine revelation that God made to Moses about the divine Identity: "God said to Moses, 'I AM WHO I AM.' He said further, 'Thus you shall say to the Israelites, "I AM has sent me to you"'" (Exod. 3:14). The movement from the beginning to the end of the Gospel pericope, then, really concerns Jesus' identity. He is no mere Jew seeking water to slake his thirst; he is the Messiah-God who gives others living water, who gives life.

Much happens in between the beginning of the passage and its ending; these are little side detours giving us greater insight into the bigger story of Jesus' identity and mission. There is the side trip about wells and buckets and natural water; Jesus speaks of giving them living water "gushing up to eternal life" (v. 14b). The Samaritan woman still doesn't get it — she wants this living water so she never has to come back to the well again. How practical! So Jesus tries another tack. He faces the woman with a fact of her life that he, a stranger, would not know: how many husbands she has had. Now the woman is beginning to move forward in the encounter and in her understanding of Jesus; she thinks Jesus is a prophet (v. 19). Then the woman comes back to the worship question; if Jesus is truly a prophet, then he would be able to see through the Samaritan-Jewish worship controversy. And he does. He assures the Samaritan woman that *place* of worship — whether Mount Ger-

izim or Jerusalem — is not the real issue, but rather that "the hour
. . . is now here" (v. 23) when worship will be in "spirit and truth"
(vv. 23b and 24b). Spirit, truth, and I AM — all three point to the
presence of God. Jesus is announcing that he is a divine Being. He
is the place of worship.

What the woman does next is quite symbolic: she leaves her
water jar and goes back to the city (v. 28). This indicates a shift in
her understanding of who Jesus is. She forgets about the well water
and now is focused on Jesus as the Living Water. Her question to
the townspeople — "He cannot be the Messiah, can he?" (v. 29b)
— functions as a rhetorical question, and her disciple-witness-
evangelization is effective because the townspeople leave the city
and go "on their way to him." They prevail upon Jesus to stay with
them, which he does, for two days (v. 40b). Now they hear Jesus
himself teach, and they come to believe in him as "the Savior of the
world" (v. 42c). Not only is the woman at the well transformed by
hearing and believing, but so is the whole town.

With this interpretation, the answer that we must worship in
"spirit and truth" is quite a good one when the phrase is understood in all its fullness. Jesus himself is "spirit and truth." Our
worship is less concerned about a place than it is concerned about a
divine Person. To worship in "spirit and truth" means that we focus
on Jesus, who gives us living water, who leads us to the Father, who
gives us the Spirit so that we might empty ourselves for the sake of
living as he did. The deepest meaning of our worship is to adhere
to Jesus as our Messiah-Savior, who leads us to the Triune God,
who is full of mercy and steadfast love. Encounters with Jesus are
encounters with our Triune God. These encounters elicit worship:
falling down in adoration before "I AM," who gives us living water
for eternal life.

Reflecting Pause

We drink thirstily from Jesus, who gives us living water, when . . .
This transforms us as a congregation in that . . .
To say that Jesus is the Messiah means to us . . .
To say that Jesus is the Savior of the world means to us . . .
To worship in spirit and truth means to us . . .
Elements of our worship which point to our worshiping in spirit
    and truth are . . .

Heavenly Worship: Multitudes Forever Sing God's Praises

We would be quite remiss if, in a discussion of God's word and worship, we did not make at least a few comments on that visionary last book of the Bible, The Revelation to John. Chapters 4 and 5 describe the heavenly worship. There is a throne, and while John's vision does not describe a figure (God) as such, he uses rich imagery of beautiful things to point to the ineffable God. The "living creatures give glory and honor and thanks to the one who is seated on the throne" (Rev. 4:9), echoing the words of the heavenly seraphs in Isaiah's call: "Holy, holy, holy" (Isa. 6:3). They also proclaim that God is worthy to receive our worship (Rev. 4:11). The next part of the vision introduces the Lamb who was slain, and they repeat their song, that the Lamb is also worthy of our worship (Rev. 5:9a, 12a), for it is he who by his "blood . . . ransomed for God" all peoples (Rev. 5:9b). To this the heavenly court says, "Amen!" (Rev. 5:14). This glimpse of heavenly worship asserts that God is the holy One who alone is worthy of our worship.

Other insights about worship abound. A great multitude is

79

in heaven worshiping God. The 144,000 (Rev. 7) is a symbolic number, a very large one. There were 12,000 sealed from each of the twelve tribes of Israel. But while large, the number is still limited. However, in verse 9 there is an unlimited multitude ("no one could count") giving the Lamb glory and honor (7:12). Jesus offers eternal life to all who remain faithful to him, those who "have washed their robes and made them white in the blood of the Lamb" (7:14c).

Chapter 19 gives us yet another glimpse of heavenly worship. Again, there is a great multitude singing God's praises. "Hallelujah!" ("Praise God!") is sounded four times (vv. 19:1b, 3b, 4c, 6c). Then there is a reversal. Those who worship are blessed: "Blessed are those who are invited to the marriage supper of the Lamb" (19:9b). We who worship God are united with God in such a way that we share in God's holiness, God's blessedness, God's eternal wedding feast. All we need do is hear Jesus say, "Come" (Rev. 22:17; the word "come" is repeated three times in this verse).

One curious detail in Revelation's account of heavenly worship occurs at the beginning of Chapter 8: "When the Lamb opened the seventh seal, there was silence in heaven for about half an hour" (Rev. 8:1). The final seal has been opened, and the brief period of silence provides a transition to the next part of the vision, the seven trumpets. This silence is a limited one — "half an hour" is not very long (but we are reminded that there is no "time" in heaven, so all these numbers are symbolic). We cannot stay with one vision; more is to come. At the same time, this brief silence gives all heaven a time to catch up with the glory of God to which the worship is directed. Without silence, even the heavenly liturgy can go amiss. We need silence to catch up with the marvelous moment that encounter with the divine One brings. Without this silence, the vision is too easily shattered, disjointed, dissipated.

The Revelation to John is a highly symbolic vision, the meaning of which is still debated by scholars. It is not our point here to interpret the whole vision. We simply want to "catch" the awe, magnitude, and inspiring character of the heavenly worship. But this kind of worship is not simply something relegated to our future. One thing the Eastern churches can teach us is that each time we come together for worship, we join our hearts and minds with the whole heavenly choir in offering God praise and honor and glory and thanksgiving. The heavenly court magnifies the limits of our own voices and hearts to an unlimited chorus of praise not bound by time and space but extending into the heavens and eternity itself.

....

Reflecting Pause

What strikes us about the heavenly worship is . . .
We feel we are numbered among the heavenly multitude giving
God honor and praise and glory and thanksgiving during our
congregation's communal worship when . . .
We feel most washed in the blood of the Lamb when . . .
We are compelled as a congregation to sing Hallelujah when . . .

....

These are not the only passages from the New Testament pertinent to coming to a deeper understanding of worship. For example, the letter to the Hebrews helps us explore our own participation in the high priesthood of Jesus Christ (Heb. 4:14–5:10; 7:1–8:13). The First Letter to Timothy lists the qualifications for bishops (1 Tim. 3:1-7) and deacons (1 Tim. 3:8-13). There are more than twenty references to prayer and worship in the book of Acts, sometimes stating a place (e.g., the synagogue or temple), sometimes a time (first, sixth, and ninth hours — that is, about six in the morning, noon, and three in the afternoon), sometimes persons who pray (e.g., Peter and Paul). But in all of this talk about prayer and worship, in both the Old and the New Testaments, what is clear is that God from the beginning has moved us humans to take a posture of reverence and awe before the divine Majesty.

From the beginning God has chosen to be present to us, inviting us to encounter the divine Majesty in our worship and prayer. From the beginning God draws us out of ourselves toward a beauty, immensity, and inclusiveness that can take our breath away. Breathless, we are filled with God's Spirit-Breath, who enables us to worship with full hearts.

CHAPTER 3

Who We Are before God:
"Do You Not Know . . . ?"

And as we rise with You to live,
O let the Holy Spirit give
The sealing unction from above,
The joy of life, the fire of love.

Adoniram Judson, "Come, Holy Spirit, Dove Divine," verse 4

ST. PAUL ASKS a very pointed question at the beginning of the sixth chapter of his letter to the Romans: "Do you not know that all of us who have been baptized into Christ Jesus were baptized into his death?" (Rom. 6:3a). This question is ever so pertinent today.

What baptism is and what it does often escape us once baptism has been celebrated. If a denomination practices infant baptism, those baptized would not even remember the ceremony. Perhaps photos can remind them that it did indeed happen. They might have these concrete traces of who was present. The happy smiles might tell them that it was a good occasion. If a denomination practices believer (adult) baptism, those baptized would naturally remember the ceremony. But all too frequently it might be relegated to the recesses of their memory, not immediately on their minds. Clearly, we have much formation to do in our congregations to help others realize that baptism is so much more than a ceremony, so much more than what makes us card-carrying Christians!

Baptism is an entrance into a way of life. It initiates us into the Christian community, conforms us to Christ, marks us as those who are saved, and gives us a new identity as members of Christ's Body. The ceremony always takes place at a certain time and in a certain place. But the reality of baptism is ongoing in our lives. Baptism is the door into a way of worshiping and living that can and must continually grow. We dare gather as a Christian community to offer God our praise and thanksgiving because we have first surrendered ourselves through baptism into God's loving arms and received from God divine life. We have given ourselves over to something larger than ourselves, something that defines who we are and why we embrace a life of Christian discipleship.

In this chapter we consider baptism as an ongoing commitment to living worshipful lives. We reflect on the saving mystery of Christ into which we are baptized. We assess who we are before God and how that shapes our worship. We want more fully and knowingly to respond to Paul's question, "Do you not know . . . ?" Only by responding to his question with all our hearts can we worship God with gladness.

Our Common Baptismal Identity

Unlike the other three Gospels, that of Mark says nothing about Jesus' birth — neither about the events surrounding his lowly birth as a baby (as in Matthew and Luke) nor about his lofty identity as the divine Word present at the beginning of creation and made flesh among us to dispel darkness and sin (John 1:1-5, 10, 14). No, Mark begins with the adult Jesus who is baptized by his cousin John in the Jordan River (Mark 1:9). Obviously, Jesus' baptism is not one of repentance for the forgiveness of sins, but instead the occasion for announcing who he is as he embarks on his public ministry. The Spirit descends on Jesus "like a dove," and his identity is revealed as God's "Son, the Beloved," in whom God is well pleased (Mark 1:10-11). Baptism initiates Jesus into a new way of ministry and of relating to others; and baptism does the same for us. The Scriptures show us two different theological ways to approach baptism, derived from two different pericopes of God's word.

The first passage we have already introduced at the beginning of this chapter: Romans 6:1-11. Paul is explaining to us that in baptism we are plunged into the death of Christ so that we might rise with him in new life. The word "baptism" comes from the Greek *baptizein*, which means "to plunge." In our own practice of baptism today, for the most part we are not plunged into flowing, baptismal waters. Many churches have renovated their baptismal spaces to include an immersion font — that is, a font that is large enough and deep enough for the person being baptized to stand or kneel in the pool, with the minister pouring a good amount of water over the person. Some churches still baptize in rivers, emulating the baptism of John in the Jordan, and actually do plunge (submerge) the individual into or under the water.

This is the way they did baptisms during the height of adult baptisms in the fourth and fifth centuries. The baptismal pool was often in the form of a sarcophagus (an elongated coffin or tomb). Usually the baptismal font would have an east-west orientation. The west (where the sun sets) symbolized the region of darkness and sin. In many early communities, the renunciation of evil would take place facing the west. Sometimes even the person being baptized would spit toward the west as a grand gesture of contempt for evil after the renunciatory part of the baptismal promises. Then the person to be baptized would be led down steps (from the west) and plunged three times into the waters (which were fairly deep) while the minister recited the Trinitarian formula commanded by Christ (Matt. 28:19).

There is some early evidence of a further detail that really brings home what happens in the water-bath. The minister would hold the person under the water long enough that he or she would begin to struggle to come up for life-giving air. At a critical moment the minister would raise up the person, who would gulp for air, then plunge him or her under for a second and then a third time. The ritual celebration brought home in a vivid way that the person was dying — to self. The person being baptized would experience actual fright about the plunging; it would feel something like the experience of dying.

After the third plunging, the person would be brought up out of the water and clothed in a white garment; then he or she would ascend from the font up the steps toward the east. The east is the region of light, of a new day. The person just baptized would now be a new person. A new day would be dawning in the person's life, a day signaling new life, new beginnings, a new way of being in community, a new identity as a member of the Body of Christ. The old self had died in those waters, and a new person had risen up, "so we too might walk in the newness of life" (Rom. 6:4c). Paul goes on in his letter to make this dying and rising mystery quite explicit:

> For if we have been united with him in a death like his, we will certainly be united with him in a resurrection like his. We know that our old self was crucified with him so that the body of sin might be destroyed, and we might no longer be enslaved to sin. For whoever has died is freed from sin. But if we have died with Christ, we believe that we will also live with him. . . . So you also must consider yourselves dead to sin and alive to God in Christ Jesus. (Rom. 6:5-8, 11)

Death is not all there is. Jesus Christ has conquered death: "Death has been swallowed up in victory. Where, O death, is your victory? Where, O death, is your sting?" (1 Cor. 15:54c, 55). The invitation of baptism is to live in the new life we have been given, not in the sinful ways of our former selves. This new life is celebrated as a new identity. It is amazing that in our own baptism the same thing happens to us as happened at Jesus' baptism: the Spirit manifests the identity of those belonging to God. By dwelling within us, the Spirit brings us a share in divine life. In turn, because we share in divine life, we too are named beloved daughters and sons of God. Baptism initiates us into a new and most intimate relationship with God, a new covenant, captured in familial language of sons and daughters, of heirs of the life Christ has gained for us.

Perhaps these baptismal events are not as dramatic in our own lives as in the scriptural and early church accounts, but they nonetheless happen and are just as real. Many of us think of our baptism as something that happened to us long ago. But our baptism is actually an ongoing daily reality in our lives whereby we live out our identity and take up Jesus' ministry. Each time we say yes to God's will, we walk with Jesus, listen to him teach us, witness his mighty deeds, and hear him invite us to follow him. We take up our journey and walk with him, walk to where each of the Gospels inevitably leads: to Jerusalem, to death and to risen life. All of the Gospels focus on Jesus and his message of Good News. Throughout our Christian journey, as we learn more deeply what it means to follow Jesus as disciples, we hear again and again God say, "You are my beloved daughter/son with whom I am well pleased" (Matt. 3:6, paraphrased).

Another, complementary approach to understanding baptism comes from the Johannine tradition. Besides being a sacrament of death and life, of being plunged into the saving mystery of Christ, baptism also is called the sacrament of regeneration or of being born again (John 3:1-8). The context for this passage is a conversation between Jesus and the Pharisee Nicodemus, who has been coming to Jesus to learn from him. Nicodemus has connected Jesus' being able to work signs (for example, the miracle of changing water to wine at the wedding feast at Cana, which is recorded in the previous chapter) with his "com[ing] from God" (3:2b). Jesus comments that "no one can see the kingdom of God without being born from above" (3:3). Nicodemus is a bit sarcastic and critical in his reply to this; how can anyone go back into his or her mother's womb and be born again? (3:4). Jesus is patient, however, and explains that the rebirth is not of the flesh, but of the Spirit (3:5-6). Through baptism we are regenerated by the Spirit into being en-Spirited.

These two approaches to baptism — tomb and womb — are not mutually exclusive. In Jesus' conversation with Nicodemus, he reveals that "just as Moses lifted up the serpent in the wilderness [Num. 21:9], so must the Son of Man be lifted up, that whoever believes in him may have eternal life" (John 3:14). Rebirth in the Spirit is made possible because of Jesus' dying and rising, because of the perfect conformity of his will to his Father's will. Both tomb and womb require a dying to self so that we can rise to new life in Christ. Without dying to self, giving ourselves over to God in a new covenant, this new life is not possible.

Baptism initiates us into a whole complex of conversion, surrender, and new life. Life in the Spirit and a new identity are given to us at the moment of baptism, but our entire life is spent living out this tremendous invitation by God to live in divine life. The new identity in Christ that baptism confers has multiple effects for us: the old self dies, and sins are forgiven; we are plunged into Christ's dying and rising mystery (the paschal mystery, explored next); we receive the life of the Holy Spirit and a *unique* gift for building up the Body of Christ; we are made members of the Body of Christ, become children of God, and heirs of eternal life; and we are given a share in Christ's high priesthood.

Because of baptism, when we gather for worship, much more is happening than merely coming together as a human community to recognize our dependence upon God and offer ourselves in praise and thanksgiving to God. We gather as individuals, but in the very surrender of self that worship requires (at least in terms of a formal Sunday service, whether that unfolds as worship or as the liturgy of the Lord's Supper), we become more than our individual selves; we make visible the Body of Christ. We bear on ourselves the very mark of Christ: we are a wounded humanity that has risen to new life. We have been given gifts for building up the Body (1 Cor. 12), gifts that are first expressed in worship but then are carried forth from worship to our homes, workplaces, and leisure spaces so that we continue to build up the Body, making the kingdom of God, the reign of God, present (a theme addressed in Chapter 4).

We usually associate "priest" with the ordained ministers who lead our worship services. In our reflection on baptism, however, we are reminded that one of the effects of baptism and our being grafted onto Christ (Rom. 11:16b-24; John 15:1-8) is that we are made sharers in Christ's high priesthood (see Heb. 4:14–5:10). As Christ — through his life and ministry, death and resurrection, and ascension and sending of the Spirit — has mediated for us a new covenant, so we mediate for each other the witness and discipline it takes to be faithful to our baptismal covenant and the kind of worship that our baptism makes possible. So we witness to each other how beloved we are in God's sight. At worship we build each other up as the Body of Christ so that we might more perfectly offer our sacrifice of praise and thanksgiving. We pray for each other so that we can be ever more faithful to God. We intercede for the needs of the community and the world so that God's reign is established.

Baptism initiates us into the life of Christ, but this initiation is a lifelong process of completion. Each time we recite a profession of faith (for example, the Apostles' Creed), we are ratifying our baptismal belief in the presence and goodness of God, the forgiveness God promises, and the identity and dignity with which we have been bestowed. Baptism is not merely a special ceremony and an occasion for a feast and gifts. It is our entry into a life of self-giving for the sake of others. It is a dying to self for the life of others. It is being reborn, regenerated, again and again in God's very gift of Self, God's very life.

At baptism we are plunged into the dying of Christ and reborn to live as the daughters and sons of God, God's very beloved. Such a mystery, this paschal dying and rising!

....

Reflecting Pause

We experience God's calling us beloved daughters and sons when . . .
We help others hear God call them this by . . .
What helps us live during the week the Good News of salvation we read/pray/hear proclaimed from God's inspired Word is . . .
What we as a congregation can do to help ourselves be more aware of our baptismal commitment is . . .
Others help us become more aware of our baptism when . . .
God is well pleased with us when . . .

....

The Saving Mystery of Christ

How do we make sense out of the terrible suffering which Hurricane Katrina brought to so many people? Or the years-long drought in Texas? Or the tsunami in Japan? How do we help a young boy understand that his father's terminal cancer is not anyone's fault and that he is not being punished by God? How do we comfort a young girl who has just been raped? How do we cope with the loss of a job due to downsizing or the loss of a home due to fire? Often our first response to these and so many other life situations is to fall back on our faith. By turning to God in prayer, we receive the strength to cope and the hope that tragedy is not all there is to life.

These difficulties of life actually do more than bring us to God (as important and wonderful as that is). They also help us to understand what worship is really all about and, ultimately, what life is all about and who we really are. How is this so? It is so because we have been grafted onto Christ and Christ's life. Because we have been initiated into the Body of Christ, we are never alone (even when it seems as though we are). Our suffering is another's; another's suffering is ours. There is great comfort in the solidarity and support we have in each another. Our baptism and Jesus' saving mystery remind us that we Christians are always passing from death into new life. We are always being regenerated into more perfect members of the Body of Christ. We are ever on our paschal ("passing over") journey toward the fullness of life that is eternal life.

Jesus' saving mystery is sometimes referred to as the "paschal mystery." This term, however, does not appear in the Scriptures at all, or even in early Christian writings. Certainly, the word "mystery" does, especially when referring to Jesus' saving mystery and our participation in it. Certainly the concept behind "paschal mystery" does, especially when considering the baptized Christian's incorporation into Christ and his saving mission. Some Christian traditions do not use the phrase "paschal mystery" as such, but instead speak in terms of union with Christ or of our being with and in Christ and Christ in us. However we refer to the mystery, we all accept that we are baptized into Christ (see Rom. 6), share in his ministry (see Matt. 28:18-20), and are gifted members of his one Body (see 1 Cor. 12).

When we use the term "paschal mystery," we usually think of Easter and our heightened celebration of Jesus' death and resurrection in the springtime of the year. That understanding of the paschal mystery is correct, but only minimally so. Jesus' "dying and rising" is a nice shorthand way of thinking about the paschal mystery, but there is so much more to his saving mystery than what happened on that first Good Friday and Easter Sunday two millennia ago. To understand more fully, we must at least go back to the Incarnation, when the Second Person of God "humbled himself, becoming obedient to death, even death on a cross" (Phil. 2:8). Then we must also consider Jesus' public ministry and how he had always done "just as the Father . . . commanded" (John 14:31). Our insights into Jesus and who he is give us insight into ourselves and who we are through our baptism. This more comprehensive understanding of the phrase "paschal mystery" is what some traditions are getting at when they refer to this mystery as our union with Christ and his being in us. So, when I use the phrase "paschal mystery" here, I am including all this richness and the ever so many other words we might use to capture Jesus' saving mystery. For convenience's sake, I use the phrase "paschal mystery" in my remarks, without intending to eliminate other ways of saying it.

The key to understanding the paschal mystery is to remember that Jesus always did his Father's will: he was the *obedient* Son from the very first breath of his human life. Armed with this perfect and firmly established relationship with his Father, Jesus willingly became "obedient to death, even death on a cross. Because of this, God greatly exalted him" (Phil. 2:8-9) by raising him up on the third day. Jesus' life is a model for us of obedience and self-giving. This already helps us understand more clearly what worship is really all about: encountering the obedient and self-giving Christ Jesus.

The hymn-poem preserved for us in the letter to the Philippians is a marvelous composition of poetic beauty, but an even more marvelous revelation of a fuller meaning of the Incarnation and who Jesus is. Let us pause for a moment to ponder that beautiful declaration: Christ "did not regard equality with God as something to be exploited" (Phil. 2:6b). The Greek word translated here as "exploited" actually means "robbery." Scholars think this rendering of the word is quite impossible in this Scripture passage — but perhaps not. The inspired poet who composed this (probably) early Christian hymn was trying to express that it was not a matter of Jesus being "robbed" of his divinity, but rather that he freely emptied himself and "separated" himself from the Godhead in order to "tak[e] the form of a slave" (2:7b). In comparison to being God, being human is "slavery" — we are encumbered with the propensity to say and do yes when we mean/want to say and do no, and say and do no when we mean/want to say and do yes (cf. Matt. 21:28-31; Rom. 7:15-26). As a human, Jesus took on this very slavery; like us, he could be tempted to do and be other than he was and is (cf. the temptation in the desert: Luke 4:1-13). The difference between Jesus and us in this regard is that Jesus always was faithful to his Father; he never compromised his identity, either as a divine Person or as the most perfect of human beings.

What enabled Jesus to be so faithful to his relationship with his Father was his humility, obedience, and self-emptying. In other words, the center of Jesus' life was not himself, but his Father in heaven. The Greek word for self-emptying is *kenosis*, and it was a way of life for Jesus. Because of this, God "highly exalted him" (Phil. 2:9a). Within this one perfect Being we have a perfect balance of *kenosis* and exaltation. This parallels and is perhaps an even richer description of the paschal mystery than dying and rising. Surely there are parallel terms here as far as the mystery of salvation goes: dying // *kenosis*; rising // exaltation. One advantage of thinking of the paschal mystery with the help of a reflection on the Philippians hymn is that it moves us beyond Good Friday and

Easter Sunday to become for us a way of living from our first breath to our last.

At the Last Supper, when Jesus commanded his disciples to "do this in memory of me" (Luke 22:19), he was telling us more than that we must simply respond to his command to eat of his Body and drink of his Blood. He was also telling us that every time we celebrate liturgy (for example, when we worship with both word and sacrament) we "do this" as making present Jesus' dying and rising, his obedience and self-giving, his *kenosis* and exaltation. The very heart of liturgy is to make present Jesus' self-giving (his dying) so that we might be transformed and become ourselves more perfectly obedient and self-giving and thus, with him, rise to new life. Just as the Incarnation gave a human identity to Jesus, so liturgy gives us a share in divine identity. In liturgy, who we are before God is a Body united with Jesus the divine Son.

The tremendous gift of liturgy — word and sacrament worship — is that the risen Christ is present to us not as a far-off God but as a Lover who embraces all our humanity (even suffering and death, everything except sin) so that we might share in his divine life. The paschal mystery, then, is not so much a concept to be understood as it is a *Person* being faithful and calling us to be faithful, a Person identifying with us so that we might identify with him. The paschal mystery is the very breath of our own lives, for, in liturgy, we ourselves are transformed ever more perfectly into obedient and self-giving followers of Christ who are called to imitate his *kenosis* so that we might share in his exaltation.

Again, Jesus' mystery becomes our own mystery at our baptism. St. Paul asks, "Do you not know that we who were baptized into Christ Jesus were baptized into his death? . . . so that . . . we too might live in newness of life" (Rom. 6:3-4). "Do you not know . . ." Unfortunately, Paul's question seems to pass us by at times. We sometimes forget how important baptism is, as we explored above.

We sometimes forget who our baptismal identity makes us before God.

We cannot say it often enough. In baptism we are plunged into death-claiming and life-giving water: we die to our old selves and are raised from the water to be anointed in the life of the Spirit. By the power of that Spirit, we come to share in God's life. Further, baptism commits us to enter into the very life which Jesus lived; as disciples, we are members of his Body and continue his saving ministry in our broken and wounded world, a world that at the same time is redeemed. When tragedy strikes, we are challenged to embrace the passion of Jesus and bring life to others. This is how we make sense of all that happens in our lives: everything is an opportunity to live Jesus' passion and through death to come to new life.

The paschal mystery — suffering and joy, dying and rising — is not a matter of "paying our dues" (suffering and dying) so that we might be "rewarded" (share in divine life). What Jesus taught us is that as his disciples we must take up our own cross and lose our lives for the sake of others (see Matt. 16:24). In this very self-giving (kenosis), we conform ourselves more perfectly to the Christ in whom we were baptized; in this very self-giving, God raises us to new life. Thus, in the very dying is the rising.

In liturgy we make present and celebrate the paschal mystery, the dying and rising of Jesus. This is probably fairly easy for most of us to accept. Perhaps more challenging for us is that the paschal mystery is also how we must live every day — the dying and rising is the very breath of our Christian living when we are being faithful followers of Jesus. It is an amazing gift, this baptismal life to which we are committed and in which we live our sorrows and joys, our weakness and grace.

No matter how we talk about it, no matter how much we ponder it, no matter how little we seem to grasp its richness, the paschal mystery remains for those of us baptized into Christ our very way of life. The challenge of our baptism is to move paschal mystery from theory to lived reality; from historical event to present experience. What beckons us onward is that we already share in risen life even as we continue dying to self; we already are exalted even as we are steeped in the demands of daily *kenosis*. Christian/gospel living is self-sacrifice for the good of others. It is paschal living. It is willingly embracing the saving mystery of Christ.

....

Reflecting Pause

We experience the "ongoingness" of our baptism when we . . .
We express this in our worship when we . . .
We experience the relationship between Christ's mystery and our
daily living in these ways:
We experience the dying and rising, kenotic and exalting rhythm
of the paschal mystery most surely when we . . .
We could best connect our baptism and our congregation's wor-
ship if we were to . . .

....

A New and Shared Vision of Worship

Communal worship can easily become something we do by rote. We are there faithfully, but sometimes in body only. For worship truly to be the center of our lives, truly to be our own expression of Christ's *kenosis* and exaltation, we must constantly be renewing ourselves in worship. We must be growing ever deeper into our identity as those baptized into Christ, those who are members of Christ's Body. Most denominations have regular meetings of key leadership to monitor the quality of church life, hold elections, and make decisions concerning the good of all the congregants. At the same time, congregations tend to assess the quality of worship, too. For Christian worship to remain vital, focused on God, celebrating our salvation in and through Christ, we must constantly strive to do better, to come to deeper insight, to strengthen our commitment to discipleship. Christian worship demands constant renewal.

This renewal of worship must go much deeper than simply rearranging the worship service, bringing in a guest preacher, augmenting the choir, changing the environment, or adding a stunning PowerPoint presentation to illustrate sermon or hymn or gospel passage. Any serious renewal of worship means that we consider what we understand worship to be, measure the spiritual growth as individuals and congregations that our worship together has brought about from year to year, and evaluate whether we are truly surrendering during worship to God's gracious presence and opening ourselves to the transformation that God wishes to bring about in us. We cannot take these issues for granted.

One exercise that congregations tend to avoid but that is absolutely necessary for worship renewal is to develop a clear vision of what our worship is to be for our particular worshiping community. This exercise cannot be an abstract one or one where we talk in generalities but never get down to specifics. It is truly helpful to have a set of written belief-statements about worship that can serve as a kind of yardstick for evaluation. Agreeing on how to complete the following statements (especially if the congregation is very large and diverse) might take months or even years. But once the work is hammered out, these statements can be an invaluable tool for worship renewal. Completing these statements individually as members of a worshiping community and also as a worship renewal committee might be the beginning of putting together a foundational worship blueprint for a whole congregation:

- At worship, we commit ourselves to . . .
- For us, what is *essential* for good worship is . . .
- In five years, where we hope to be with respect to our worship is . . .
- Where our worship tends to be unsatisfying is . . .
- If an "outsider" would observe us worshiping, they would say that our worship is . . .
- The meaning of "celebration" with respect to good worship is . . .

Different denominations might well come up with other pertinent things to consider, especially as they would relate to particular worship doctrine or commitments. The point here is that the more concretely we can describe our worship, our vision for it, and areas for improvement, the better the ideas we will have with respect to worship renewal. In this way we can begin with one or another point, initiate non-threatening but important changes, and then evaluate. We do not have to change our entire worship pattern — in fact, it probably would not be a good idea to do so. Worship renewal is a long and gradual process.

Obviously, the six statements above about worship renewal are not hammered in stone — only God hammers commandments into stone! Worship renewal means that the statements will need to be revisited time and time again, updated, enhanced, and sometimes even changed rather drastically as new insight is gained and new worship experiences take place that lead the congregation deeper into God's presence.

When worship renewal happens in a congregation, it breathes new life, new enthusiasm, and new meaning into the worship experience. Worship renewal breathes new life into those who are striving to follow Christ, those who are identified with him in his saving mission. Now, can we imagine what kind of renewal might occur if this envisioning would happen beyond one local congregation, taking hold within a whole worship tradition?

One such instance of this kind of worship renewal happened in the Roman Catholic Church through the Second Vatican Council (1962-1965). When Pope John XXIII called for a council in 1959, his desire was to open up the windows and let fresh air into a church that he felt needed to be brought more relevantly into the twentieth (now twenty-first!) century. But what is interesting is that the Council ended up to be more than just an event for the Catholic Church — it became a world event. Its proceedings were reported on the national nightly news. The breath of fresh air that was renewing one church became a breath of fresh air that had the potential to renew all of Christian practice. What other single religious convocation (which unfolded in a number of sessions) has held the attention of so many people for so many years? The sixteen official documents that were promulgated by the Council were (and still are) read, studied, and implemented not only by Roman Catholics, but also by many other Christian churches across our world. The documents challenged who we were before God. They still challenge us.

The very first document to be passed by the Council was the Constitution on the Sacred Liturgy (*Sacrosanctum Concilium*) on December 4, 1963. This document did not come out of a vacuum. Beginning already in the middle of the nineteenth century in some Benedictine monasteries in Europe, but really gaining momentum after the beginning of the twentieth century, was the liturgical movement. This historical endeavor had contributions from both Catholic and Protestant scholars and pastors. During this time, many historical studies were undertaken, especially research into the worship of the early church. Because of these studies, we began to think in terms of the essentials of worship, see continuity and discontinuity in worship traditions, discern where all of us had perhaps strayed a bit too far from the early church's vision of worship and its connection with the mystery of Jesus Christ. All of this scholarly and pastoral study and reflection fed into the vision of the Constitution on the Sacred Liturgy and continued in the work after the Council. The decades after the Council were a time of worship renewal that included experimentation, change, ecumenical sharing, and joint learning — all marked by a new tolerance of and an appreciation for one another. The Constitution on the Sacred Liturgy became a stimulus for worship renewal for numerous congregations and traditions.

Some of the document's vision rings so true to what is most fundamental to worship that the insights quickly became common table talk. Words and phrases like "paschal mystery," "participation," "celebration," "Body of Christ," "lectionary," and many others crept into the everyday vocabulary of ordinary Christians. As we developed an ecumenically common worship vocabulary, we began to drop the emphasis on what makes the various Christian churches different and focus more on what we share in common. We developed a new sensitivity to each other, a greater sensitivity to our commonly shared tradition, and an eagerness to worship together. The Constitution on the Sacred Liturgy can be so helpful for so many different Christian congregations because its real focus is not at all on "how to," but on the principles that are essential for Christian worship renewal. It is these principles of renewal — of laying out what Christian worship is — that make the Constitution such a fruitful resource for worship renewal across denominational boundaries.

Although many issues still divide the various Christian denominations and communions, we have a new energy toward unity that brings a new hope that the divisions will one day be healed and we can witness not only in our charity but also in our common worship that we are the one church of Christ, the one Body of Christ. We can more fully witness to the common identity we share as those baptized into the saving mystery of Christ.

Paschal Mystery in the Constitution on the Sacred Liturgy

The most important and overarching principle in the Constitution is that the paschal mystery is made present and celebrated during liturgy. At the very beginning of its introduction, the Constitution states a most basic principle: that in liturgy the mystery of Christ is expressed — a mystery that is also to be lived and is to manifest the presence of Christ's church in our world (no. 2; this is a numbering system used in official documents of the Catholic Church).

Chapter 1 of the Constitution lays out general principles governing liturgy, and begins with a rather lengthy discussion of the paschal mystery. It categorically states that redemption is accomplished by the paschal mystery (no. 5), a task Christ understood well because he was sent by his Father and he was filled with the Holy Spirit. This is also the work of Christ's disciples, who are grafted onto the paschal mystery of Christ by baptism. Throughout its long tradition, the church has always celebrated the paschal mystery, in which the victory of Christ is proclaimed (no. 6).

It is important to note here that by uniting the paschal mystery so closely with liturgy, the Constitution is not saying that liturgy is only about Christ. Liturgy is always Trinitarian, but Christ is our Great High Priest who mediates salvation for us. The fruit of liturgy and its celebration of the paschal mystery is the faithful's unity in Christ, a unity that brings the people to holiness (no. 10) and brings into sharp focus our identity as members sharing in the one Body of Christ. We celebrate liturgy in the unity of the Holy Spirit, the presence of the risen Christ among us. Further, our union with Christ and his mystery is a union with the Father. If Jesus is the *way* to the Father (cf. John 14:6), then the paschal mystery is the *means* by which we are united with Christ so closely that we are also united with the Father.

Since Sunday is the day of resurrection, it is also the day on which we reach for the fullness of the life promised by the paschal mystery (no. 106). This is why in the early church Sunday was often referred to as the "eighth day." It is a day out of time, a day when we take the "time" to celebrate that we already share in the risen life of Christ. This is why Sunday is the day *par excellence* for worship.

Liturgy in the Rhythm of the Whole Christian Life

Liturgy celebrates the in-breaking of the mystery of Christ in the here and now. The paschal mystery is not simply a past historical event, but an ongoing expression of our Good Shepherd's drawing us into himself unto eternal life. By calling liturgy the source (fount) and summit of the church's activity (cf. no. 10), the Constitution is placing liturgy at the very center of our lives. We are dismissed from liturgy to live what we have celebrated, to *be* what we have celebrated. At the same time, each day we hunger for the rest and celebration of Sunday, so every day is directed toward Sunday as well as flows from it. The whole Christian life, then, is a rhythm of liturgy (worship) and life (baptismal living).

Thus the paschal mystery captures and expresses a rhythm for our lives. On the one hand, the paschal mystery unfolds as a rhythm of *kenosis* and exaltation, of dying and rising. This is true within the very essence of the mystery itself. On the other hand, the paschal mystery invites a rhythm for the way we live each week. Six days a week we work, as did God at the very beginning of creation. But then on the seventh day (the first day of the week, "Son"-day, for us Christians), we cease our work and simply enjoy the gifts that God has given us. Thus there is a weekly rhythm of work and rest, of discipleship and Beloved, of doing and being.

THE CELEBRATION OF THE WHOLE BODY

Liturgy is not a spectator sport (see no. 48 in the Constitution on the Sacred Liturgy)! We cannot be couch potatoes during liturgy. Every person who gathers to worship is to be actively involved in celebrating; the whole Body celebrates (no. 26). Even if the pastor is leading a prayer, a lay reader is proclaiming the word of God, and the choir is singing an anthem, those in the assembly who are not directly involved in the worship elements nonetheless are not passive in the celebration. The pastor may lead a prayer, but it is the prayer of the congregation; he or she gives voice to what is in the heart of everyone present. The lay reader may be proclaiming the Scriptures, but the congregants are active hearers who internalize God's word as their own. The choir may be singing, but the whole congregation joins them in spirit to raise their hearts to God.

Many congregations have various structures that increase the hands-on involvement of congregants in the worship service. Worship-service planning committees and worship commissions are common. Some pastors meet with a small group of congregants (youth respond very well to this challenge) at the beginning of the week to reflect on the liturgical readings for the next Sunday service and prepare together the sermon or homily. Some music directors rotate small groups of choir members to help select music for services. Use of a lectionary with a schema of readings over a three-year cycle not only increases the amount of Sacred Scripture proclaimed at the weekly celebration, but also guards against the choice of Scripture being left to the desires (or even whims) of one or two persons.

All of these practical ways of having more input from more congregants about the shape and content of a worship service are about more than simply giving people a good feeling about contributing to worship. These practices are ways of bringing home the belief that worship belongs to no one individual but to the whole Body of Christ. This great involvement has an added advantage of helping congregants have a greater sensitivity to each other and differing worship needs. Worship is not about satisfying individuals; it is about surrendering ourselves as the Body of Christ to God's desires for us. The sense of community that is built up by the active preparation of many congregants for worship is a concrete sign of the unity of the Body and of worship belonging to the whole church, not just to certain individuals.

FULL, CONSCIOUS, AND ACTIVE PARTICIPATION

There is probably no other principle quoted more often from the Constitution on the Sacred Liturgy than its call for full, conscious, and active participation by all in the liturgy (see especially no. 14, but also nos. 30 and 48). It seems like more than Catholics have heard this challenge and have responded with attempts to bring about a more lively and welcoming worship experience — one much more "user friendly." Most denominations have introduced more contemporary music, drama, visual arts, dance, and other full-body, hands-on worship elements. In all of this, our hearts are in the right place: we want our worship services to touch the individuals who come, facilitate an encounter with the Divine, overflow in praise and thanks, and make a difference in the way we live. There remains a question, however: What did the Constitution on the Sacred Liturgy really have in mind when it spoke to a new way to participate in liturgy?

Many if not most Christian denominations are struggling with what lies underneath this call for full, conscious, and active participation. It simply will not do to have people come to church and be bumps on a log. Many churches are trying to introduce intergenerational worship services in an effort to get the young people more involved and interested in worship. We are concerned that our young people do not seem to take to established worship patterns. We are scrambling for solutions to the battle between contemporary worship style and traditional worship style. At the same time, "participation" in liturgy actually raises some deep issues to which we must attend if we continue on our journey of seeking a fuller meaning of what worship is. These issues have to do directly with how we are before God at worship. Some of these issues become clearer as we reflect on what it means to participate in liturgy fully, consciously, and actively. We will take some extended time here for this reflection because it is so vitally important for wholesome worship.

No fewer than five paragraphs ("paragraph" can actually include more than one grammatical paragraph) in the Constitution of the Sacred Liturgy address the issue of participation by all of the congregation in the liturgical experience. Only one paragraph, however, uses the complete phrase "full, conscious, and active participation" (no. 14). One other uses "full, active participation," thus repeating two out of the three adjectives used in no. 14 (see no. 41). In all other cases, the Constitution refers only to "active" participation (see nos. 27, 30, and 50). Perhaps the most interesting paragraph is no. 30, which even lists elements of the envisioned active participation: everyone actively participates through acclamations, responses, psalms, antiphons, hymns, actions, gestures, bodily attitudes, and reverent silence.

This brief survey of data from the Constitution raises a simple question: What, really, is intended when we speak of liturgical participation? To approach an "answer" to this question (since we are dealing with mystery, there can be no definitive answer!), we first explore the three synonyms used to describe participation in no. 14 of the Constitution. Are they really synonyms, three similar words the Constitution is using to drive home an important point?

Is it simply a fluke of the Constitution that only one paragraph mentions all three adjectives for participation? It would seem that exploring each of these three words might give us deeper insight into what is truly demanded by liturgical participation. And perhaps we will be surprised at the depth and richness of this phrase "full, conscious, and active participation," and we will begin to understand why it is so often quoted.

"Active" Participation

We begin our reflection in reverse order intentionally. As noted above with the worship elements/activities listed in no. 30, one understanding of participation does unfold at the level of *actively engaging* all those who are present in the worship experience. It would not do to have a choir sing all the hymns; at some point the whole congregation must be invited to open their hearts to God in full-throated song. It would not do to have a priest or a minister lead the worship service in such a manner that it is clear that *he or she* is doing the worship and the rest are there to watch; worship leadership cannot function apart from those who are being led — namely, the whole congregation. In a slightly different vein, it would not do to use only one's head in a worship service. The Constitution's no. 30 also makes it clear that the *whole body* must be engaged in liturgy. Particularly interesting is the inclusion of attitudes and silence in this list of active worship elements.

First, let's attend to attitude. Sometimes we are not aware of how our attitude affects others. If I am bored, this rubs off; if I am angry, this rubs off; if I am enthusiastic, this rubs off; if I am grateful, this rubs off; if I am filled with praise, this rubs off; if I am genuinely concerned for others when I make intercession, this rubs off; if I am committed to being there, this rubs off. All this makes a difference not only by affecting others' ability to participate, but also by affecting how we are as the church, the Body of

Christ. It affects who we are before God. If one member slacks off in participation, two things simultaneously happen: first, the Body is weakened; and second, the others who are participating lift up that slacker. Thus, the attitude of congregants actually is one of give-and-take.

Second, let's attend to silence. We might think of silence as a time to do nothing, to vegetate. However, the inclusion of "silence" in the list of elements of active participation suggests otherwise. In the silence, something is to happen *actively*. Silence, in other words, is a time to *do something* (pray, contemplate, encounter) and to *be someone* (a creature who is still, quiet before the Creator). Ironically, the moments of silence which we build into our worship services may well become the most engaging, active form of participation! All too often our worship is very busy, filled with movement and sounds. The Constitution reminds us that silence is an important part of worship, for it affords us the space just to *be* before God. In this interval of stillness, we discover who we are because we are able to encounter the God who chooses to be present to us. Silence and stillness during key moments of liturgy are transition points into a deeper encounter with the Sacred. Rather than passive inactivity, these moments may just well be the most active of the entire service!

"Active" participation challenges us to get involved, to be engaged, to *do* liturgy, to *work*. And this is true even if we do not feel like it, if we think we cannot sing, if we believe we have nothing really to contribute to the whole worship experience. Members of the Body of Christ affect each other. And this is very good. If on some day I am weighed down by the cares of life, then the enthusiastic, active participation of those around me may pull me into the service in such a way that for those few minutes I am able to forget my cares and give myself over to God. If on some day I am overjoyed at the birth of a baby in my family, then my joy will most probably be infectious and touch someone else who perhaps is at worship with a sad heart. Active participation not only swells the singing, gives louder voice to the prayer, introduces greater profundity to the silences, and encourages another to listen more intently — active participation also is the communal act by which we express our solidarity with each other and our unity in the Body of Christ. Active participation is an expression of how we are before God as a community.

"Conscious" Participation

The challenge to "conscious" participation occurs only once in the Constitution (no. 14), but this does not make it something unimportant or unworthy of our serious reflection. As the word "conscious" implies, we are speaking here of awareness, of deliberate effort, something a bit different from the "active" participation discussed above. The very word "conscious" derives from the Latin noun *conscius*, which means "having a common knowledge with another, to be privy to." This etymology suggests, first, that conscious participation involves more than ourselves. In fact, in the very call to worship we are invited to gather and present ourselves before the Lord — ultimately to say *yes* to the divine activity in which we are about to engage ourselves. "Conscious" participation requires of us a *surrender* of ourselves to the worship event, a surrender of ourselves to embrace the saving mystery of Christ, a surrender of ourselves to become more than we are by ourselves.

A second implication of the etymology is this: since "conscious" is a *common* knowledge, even our yes, our surrender is possible only because of the others who are present with us at worship. We can become privy to divine presence only when we surrender ourselves to the larger action, which is not what we as individuals do, but what God does in us — all of us. The very word "liturgy" comes from two Greek words meaning "the people's work." The real work of worship is not so much our active participation (as challenging and demanding as that may well be) as it is the work of *surrendering* ourselves to God's presence and God's action.

Most importantly, this surrender means that we let go of our individuality — with our likes and dislikes, our needs and desires — and surrender ourselves to be the Body of Christ at worship. Conscious participation in terms of common knowledge is not something that takes place in our heads; it is not a matter of gaining a new insight. Rather, common knowledge takes place in our hearts through our surrender to being people other than our individual selves — our surrender to being the visible, worshiping Body of Christ.

"Conscious" participation challenges us to surrender to being the Body of Christ where God works through us and within us. Conscious participation is more than active participation; it requires us to give of ourselves, to unite ourselves with the *kenosis* of Christ so that God can work in and through us for the good of all.

"Full" Participation

Two paragraphs of the Constitution mention "full" participation (nos. 14 and 41) but give us little clue about what the document intends. We might take our cue from our previous two reflections. Active engagement and conscious surrender both take us beyond ourselves. As aspects of our liturgical participation, they open us for God to work within us. Full participation, then, has to do with how God does work within us: God *transforms* us through the worship event into being more perfect members of the Body of Christ. Our full participation requires us to be open to and receptive of how God is transforming us, to be open to and receptive of how God draws us more deeply into divine life, the life that changes us.

Worship involves a bi-directional giving. We give God ourselves in praise and thanks; God gives us the divine Self as a share in divine life, which transforms us into an ever-deepening identity as

God's beloved daughters and sons. Participation reaches its apex when God transforms us and we respond with an openness to that transformation. God never forces transformation on us nor forces us to receive divine life. Divine life is pure gift; we must freely receive that gift. Thus, liturgy is always a life-threatening experience: through our engagement and surrender God makes us other than who we were when we began liturgy. Interestingly enough, while we often think of liturgy as what we give God, full participation implies that the most important gift of liturgy is what God gives to us. This does not mean that our gifts are unimportant — either of the offering or of ourselves — for they are important! It does mean that God, who receives our sincere and true gifts, transforms them with divine life and most graciously gives them back to us abundantly.

Moreover, this transformation of ourselves in liturgy is not simply for our own sake. Indeed, this transformation is precisely what enables us to be sent forth from worship to transform our broken and fractured world just as we ourselves have been transformed. Full participation, then, thrusts us toward mission. We are transformed in order to continue Jesus' saving ministry. "Full" participation challenges us to be transformed by God into ever more perfect members of the Body of Christ; as we are transformed, so is our world transformed.

Perhaps a word of caution is in order here. Our transformation by God that is proper to this understanding of full participation is not necessarily measurable or noticeable. We do not walk out the church doors, take a look at ourselves, and discover what is different about us and who we are. Probably the transformation is most noticeable in the way we live. If, after weeks of faithful worshiping, we and others identify us as more loving, more forgiving, more merciful, more generous, and more self-giving, then this is the ultimate witness to the gradual transformations that happen within us. God tends not to hit us over the head or upend us. God works in us in mysterious and usually imperceptible ways. But work in us, God does do. Full participation, then, is both God's transforming us and our living out of this new way to be before God and others. If we do not live the transformation, then it has not really happened.

This reflection on a broader meaning for "full, conscious, and active participation" helps us realize that worship is far more than doing, as important as that is. This kind of participation leads us from doing to *being* the Body of Christ, fully conscious of our encounter with the Divine and open to and receptive of the action the Divine takes on our behalf. This is ultimately the source of our deepest praise and thanksgiving — what God continues to do in and through us. This is God's continuing saving mystery.

There is a progression from one aspect of participation to another (which is why we began this reflection with "active" participation). Perhaps this schema will help us to grasp this progression clearly:

Active participation $\rightarrow$ *engagement* in worship elements

Conscious participation $\rightarrow$ *surrender* of self to liturgical action

Full participation $\rightarrow$ *reception* of being transformed by God and our living out of our new selves

We may tend to see this as a linear progression (from active to conscious to full participation), but it does not quite work this way. These are not deliberate steps we take, one after another. At the same time, without total engagement of self, surrender is hardly possible. If we do not surrender ourselves into God's hands, the reception of the transformation that God does in us by way of gift is not as apparent in our everyday living and decisions. God's actions are never dependent upon our choices; God's grace is always freely given. Active, conscious, and full participation in worship opens us to God's presence and gifts. This kind of participation frees us so that God can freely act within us.

In order for participation in worship to be fully realized, we surrender ourselves to being the Body of Christ (can we say this often enough?). This means that there are *ecclesial* (church) implications for what takes place at any given worship service. The church is at once the Body of Christ made visible in our world today and the way Christ continues his saving ministry. Full, conscious, and active participation, then, always leads us to mission on behalf of others. This kind of participation always takes us beyond ourselves and the gifts God bestows on each and every one of us, to the realization that we are all brothers and sisters in Christ. When another is in need, I am in need. When another is hurting, I am hurting. When another is encouraged, I am encouraged. When another is graced, I am graced.

As all of us Christians come to a more full, conscious, and active participation in our own separate churches, perhaps we will also come to a greater realization that in Christ we are all made one. The Constitution on the Sacred Liturgy, with its challenge to full, conscious, and active participation, has the potential to draw us together as one Body in the one saving ministry of Christ. Ultimately, our full, conscious, and active participation is a way we are before God and each other. It is a way that we live out our baptismal conformity to Christ, an identity that sets us apart as God's beloved daughters and sons.

....

Reflecting Pause

Of the challenges for worship renewal found in the Constitution on the Sacred Liturgy, the one with which we are most comfortable is . . .

The one that leaves us most uncomfortable is . . .
We experience the rhythm of the paschal mystery at worship
    most completely when . . .
The summit and source of our lives as individuals and as a con-
    gregation tends to be . . .
We are best able to come to full, conscious, and active participa-
    tion at worship when we . . .

. . . .

When we claim that baptism is the door into worship, it is no small claim we are making! Baptism transforms us into being members of the Body of Christ, the church. Our celebration of liturgy continues that transformation. We are never finished. We are always growing deeper into God's holiness and life. We are always being invited into an ever-deeper participation in the mystery of Christ's passing through death to risen life. When St. Paul asks us, "Do you not know . . . ?" it is no easy question with an easy, once-and-for-all answer. Our identity is never fully revealed, never fully finished. We are constantly growing into who we are and are becoming.

"Do you not know . . . ?" is a loaded, comprehensive question that plunges us into the depths of dying and rising, *kenosis* and exaltation, surrender and transformation. It is the question that brings us up short in the face of the incredible dignity that God offers us. The Son humbled himself to take on our humanity, and his act of obedience and response to his loving Father makes possible our own being raised up in the Holy Spirit to share in nothing less than divine life. Such a gift God gives us! To such an act of profound worship and awe this double movement of humility and exaltation brings us!

CHAPTER 4

Being Together before God: Is Worship Making a Difference in How We Live?

Forth in thy name, O Lord, I go,
My daily labor to pursue;
Thee, only thee, resolved to know
In all I think or speak or do.

Charles Wesley, "Forth in Thy Name, O Lord, I Go," verse 1

JESUS TELLS HIS hearers that we are to *go* not only one mile for others, but two (Matt. 5:41). The Twelve are told to *go* and proclaim the Good News (Matt. 10:7; Mark 16:15; Luke 9:60). Before his ascension, Jesus commissioned his disciples to *go* and make disciples of all nations (Matt. 28:19). The risen Jesus tells the women who have come to the tomb to anoint him to *go* and tell his disciples to *go* to Galilee, where they will see him (Mark 16:7; John 20:17). Jesus resolutely sets out to *go* to Jerusalem and his passion and death (Luke 9:51). Peter naïvely declares that he is prepared to *go* even to prison and death to follow Jesus (Luke 22:33). After Jesus raises Lazarus, the bystanders are told to unbind him and let him *go* (John 11:44c). From at least the fourth century onward, Christians have been sent forth from worship with the Latin imperative *ite* — "*go*." The complete phrase used for dismissal was *Ite, missa est* — "*missa*" being a past participial form of the Latin verb *mitto*, *mittere*, "to send." Christians do not live a passive faith; they do not sit around waiting for something to happen to them. Jesus himself makes clear that we are to be evangelizers, that we are to *go* out and proclaim the gospel, the Good News.

The context for being sent to proclaim, however, is not our own selves, our own insights, our own interpretations (although some of that may be part of Christian discipleship). The context is the lived experience of the risen Christ and our worship of God. Ours is a shared faith: our proclamation derives from the Christian community, from our solidarity as the Body of Christ. In this way our proclamation of the Good News is not *our* proclamation but Jesus' proclamation. We become the instruments — the mediators, the "priests" — who speak Jesus' words, do his deeds, love with his kind of love.

It would seem that from the very beginning of formal Christian worship there was a dismissal (for practical reasons), but this dismissal had an import beyond getting people out the doors. Worship cannot be contained within walls, but bursts out in two ways: in making a difference in the daily living of the worshipers, and in compelling worshipers to speak (by word and deed) the Good News. We are a community of believers; our following Jesus is never a solitary journey. The basis for this assertion is our baptismal identity as the Body of Christ. When we act, the whole Body acts. When we are sent, the whole Body is sent. When we speak, the whole Body speaks. Christ works through us to continue his saving mission (an English word derived from the same Latin verb, *mittere*).

This final chapter of our extended reflection on the meaning of worship takes us outside the sacred space to the marketplace. We consider here the many dimensions of Matthew's startling revelation about God's final judgment: when we feed the hungry, we feed

Christ; when we welcome the stranger, we welcome Christ; when we clothe the naked, we clothe Christ; when we care for the sick, we care for Christ; when we visit the imprisoned (or the elderly or homebound), we visit Christ (Matt. 25:31-46). Worship takes us outside of ourselves to others.

Worship Bursting out the Doors

To be a worshiping people does not mean that we simply get ourselves to services on Sunday; rather, worship is a way of living. Worship makes demands on us. The challenge for the future of worship renewal is to make sure these demands are more perfectly met in our daily living. Christian worship implies embracing a spirituality — that is, a way of life flowing to and from worship.

The vision of worship bursting out the doors is as old as Jesus' using saliva — the very stuff of his body — to cure a blind man (Mark 8:23; John 9:6), as inclusive as Jesus' inviting a tax collector to be an apostle and eating with sinners (Matt. 9:9-10), and as demanding and consequence-laden as Jesus' sweating blood in Gethsemane over his struggle to do the Father's will (Luke 22:42, 44). Saying this, though, surely is no guarantee that we Christians have grasped the truth of worship bursting out the doors to any great degree or depth. This is not necessarily a negative judgment of the Christian community. It does point to the mystery of which we speak. And, as we all know, mysteries are fathomless.

What does it mean to be a worshiping church bursting out the doors? Essentially, in this statement we avow our Christian being (identity) and doing (mission) — *being* (through our baptism we are made members of the Body of Christ) and *doing* (with baptism comes the bidding to be disciples and take up the ministry of Jesus). Baptism, in other words, is not just a matter of *our own* salvation; it is also about being and becoming for others the presence of the risen Christ in our redeemed but still broken world. The Incarnation of Jesus was a new and unprecedented theophany (divine manifestation) of God; baptism is also a new and unprecedented theophany — *our* being gifted with the new life that is a share in divine life by which *we* are transformed for mission. Theophany always offers new life. The challenge is to encounter, recognize, and accept. We do this during worship (hopefully!), but it cannot stay there. Encounter with God always compels a response, and this response always includes the good of others.

These statements are simple enough; at the same time, we have an inkling that there is more here than meets the eye. No theology can exhaust the richness of Christ's mystery, and no life can completely embrace the expansiveness of its grace. If, in the end, we have grasped the challenges of living our baptismal identity and mission and we truly have strived to become, ever more perfectly, members of the Body of Christ, then Jesus' saving mission is real and ongoing in our world today. A number of challenges face us as we celebrate the kind of worship that bursts out the doors.

THE FIRST CHALLENGE: INCREASED UNDERSTANDING AND LIVING OF THE SAVING MYSTERY OF CHRIST

In Chapter 3 we spent time reflecting on the saving mystery of Christ (the paschal mystery). Here we want to revisit that reflection, but in this particular context of being sent.

The twentieth-century liturgical movement, as we noted, awakened us to the paschal mystery as being at the heart of liturgy and Christian living. We have only begun to explore this important awakening. Vatican II's "back to the sources" challenged all of us to return to patristic (early church) sources. It is interesting that the phrase "paschal mystery" does not appear in any of the early sources as such. But its meaning permeates everything that is said about worship and Christian living. Therefore, one clear pastoral challenge is to help people go beyond paschal mystery as "a time of year" (Easter time) and grasp the paschal mystery as enacted in *every* liturgy and as that rhythm of dying and rising, of *kenosis* and exaltation which we are called to live each day. The most profound proclamation we make is not by the words we speak, but by the way we live. If others *see* our self-giving, we have made a profound gospel statement. If others are touched by our *joy* as new beings sharing in Christ's risen life, we have been a profound witness to the Resurrection.

With liturgy and the liturgical year there is always a pervasive danger of historicizing Christ's saving activity. We do not want to deny that it *was* a historical event completed in chronological time, but to leave it there is to rob ourselves of perhaps its greatest implication — finding *ourselves* in the mystery as vital participants in its very unfolding in the here and now. We have sometimes perpetuated a theology that has seen Christ's saving mystery in terms of "winning" or "earning" our salvation, and what we do is tap into the wealth of graces that Jesus gained for us. At best this makes us largely passive recipients: we cooperate with God's grace of salvation by engaging in communal worship, praying, leading morally good lives, and so on. But there is a different way to look at the Incarnation, salvation, and worship that has not yet caught up with too many people sitting in the chairs or pews.

Let's begin at ground zero: the paschal mystery fundamentally concerns dying and rising. (*Kenosis* and exaltation is probably a better way of saying it, but we will continue to use the more familiar "dying and rising.") From this, let's first describe the paschal mystery as a *dialectic* — of two opposite poles being in dynamic tension — of dying and rising. From our purview of dialectic, we are suggesting that the "dying" is not finished but continues as the dialectical counterpart of the rising. Even though the historical event of Jesus' death happened and was completed as a historical event in chronological time, we might suggest that even with Christ the "dying" wasn't "concluded" in that the marks of the wounds remained on the risen Lord (see John 20:27). Now, a second dialectic: the paschal mystery also comprises a dialectic of Christ and ourselves. From this double dialectic purview, we are asserting that we are *essential* participants in the paschal mystery. The point is that the paschal mystery challenges us, *first*, to graft our lives onto Christ's. *Then* we enter into living the dying and rising. At Jesus' baptism, his identity ("beloved Son") and mission ("hear him," spoken at his transfiguration) were announced; at our own baptism, we become adopted daughters and sons of God and members of Christ's Body, becoming his disciples. Faithful mission and discipleship mean surrendering our own wills so that we do God's will. This surrender (self-emptying obedience to hearing and doing God's will) is what plunges us into the dying and rising mystery.

To be sure, this surrender, the kenotic self-emptying of surrender, always leads to transformation, ongoing conversion. It is this transformation and conversion that mark our being more perfectly grafted onto Christ and enable us to go deeper and deeper into the riches of paschal-mystery worship and living. Being faithful disciples always involves dying to self. Of course, "dying" is used equivocally here. It can mean our definitive death as humans — the end of our earthly lives. Or, practically, it also means all those daily "dyings" in which we submit our will to God's — that is, dying to self for the sake of others. Even with respect to Jesus, we usually think of paschal-mystery dying as his death on the cross; we sometimes forget that Jesus died daily, too (e.g., the crowds pressed around him, his hearers did not understand his message of Good News, and he was constantly being challenged and questioned by the authorities). At the same time, we Christians know with unfailing certainty that dying always leads to new life, because Christ has shown us the way.

By our surrendering to and embracing dying to self, God's reign is manifest; Jesus ascended to take his rightful place at the Father's right hand, and we already share in the glory of divine life. Jesus' mission here on earth was completed (marked by the Ascension) at the same time that (with Pentecost) it became our own mission as disciples of Jesus. Accordingly, there is a "not yet" aspect to the mystery in that we are still passing from sinfulness to sinlessness at the same time that we "already" share in divine life.

Explaining the paschal mystery in this dialectical way underscores the ongoing nature of Christ's saving act and how each one of us through baptism is plunged into the saving mystery of Christ. The key here is *being* and *doing*. Our identity is as the Body of Christ, and being so one with Christ means that Christ's mission is our mission. It is not another mission, but the same mission. Consequently, we are a worshiping community sent forth for far deeper reasons than that we get ourselves out of a church service — we are a worshiping church being sent because of our *very identity and mission* as the Body of Christ. As St. Augustine said long ago in Sermon 272 (cf. also Sermon 227), Eucharist is who we are:

If you are the Body of Christ and members of it, then it is that mystery which is placed on the Lord's table: you receive the mystery, which is to say the Body of Christ, your very self. You answer Amen to who you are, and in the answer you embrace yourself. You hear Body of Christ and answer Amen. Be a member of Christ's body, that your amen will be true. (translation by the author)

Of course, for anything at all to happen at worship, it must be celebrated well. This suggests our second challenge.

THE SECOND CHALLENGE:
CELEBRATING WORSHIP WELL

Any number of pastoral challenges come to the fore in a discussion about celebrating worship well. First of all, we must get beyond attending worship simply out of obligation (although the precept to worship is one of the Ten Commandments). We are drawn to worship each Sunday because it is the day of resurrection. Our hunger for an encounter with God leads us to worship. Our concern for others leads us to worship as the fount and source of all the good we do every day. Sunday worship is the time when we surrender to and experience the dying and rising that also characterize our Christian living. Thus worship is inherently hope-filled, because when dying and rising are radically topsy-turvy in our everyday living (most often because we experience all "dying"), worship reminds us of the new life that inevitably is ours when we surrender to dying to self. We *need* Sunday worship in order to keep our lives in balance. We *need* Sunday worship in order to remind ourselves that the dying we experience *always* leads to rising. We *need* the brief respite from daily cares that worship can offer in order to gain the strength and perspective to feed the hungry, clothe the naked, visit the lonely, smile at the service clerk, be patient with the children.

Another challenge for worshiping well is to understand exactly what it is we are doing when we gather. Expansively put, we are *enacting* (not *reenacting*, which can speak of "historicization" of the mystery) the life and saving mystery of Christ, even though on a given Sunday this may be a small part of the whole. This suggests that the "celebration" of worship cannot be judged simply by whether congregants experience an affective "high," nor can that be the objective of the celebration (although there is nothing wrong when that happens!). Good celebration always demands a surrender of self so that a transforming encounter with God can take place. Full, conscious, and active participation always leads to being transformed by God into more perfect members of the Body of Christ.

If we begin from the stance that liturgy enacts the saving mystery of Christ, then all elements of the liturgy must serve this fundamental function. When people who say "That was a great liturgy!" are asked why, most often their response centers on either great music or great preaching. But good worship demans far more than this. Good worship requires careful preparation and good leadership. Already in the New Testament writings we hear qualifications for the community and liturgical leadership, qualifications that rest in a community knowing the individual (see 1 Tim. 3:1-5 and Titus 1:5-9). In the early strata of church history, faithful discipleship determined the rule of practice and leadership; later, church rule of practice determined leadership, and proven faithful discipleship all too often receded into the background.

Finally, another challenge for celebrating worship well is that the various liturgical ministers must be better formed, more knowledgeable about what they are doing. Often even the liturgical leadership in a congregation (ministers or priests, worship planners, worship commission members, musicians) have only limited notions about a theology of worship or the purpose of worship. Nor can we take for granted that the average person in the pew (or liturgical leadership, for that matter) grasps even the simplest notions about worship. This need for worship education is such an important point that we discuss it as the third challenge.

THE THIRD CHALLENGE:
ENGAGING WORSHIP EDUCATION

It is one thing to assert that liturgy enacts the paschal mystery; it is quite another thing to assert that those celebrating liturgy truly grasp what this means. There is no substitute for continued education about our worship, what it means, what it means to each of us individually, and how we are to live it. Sometimes new worship elements or practices are introduced at the weekly service, but there has been no real explanation of why or what they mean. Introducing change simply for novelty's sake does not serve well the basic purpose of worship: to give God praise and thanks for all the great deeds God has done on our behalf. At the same time, we all know that when education programs are offered in our congregations, often only a handful of people avail themselves of the opportunity. Adult education techniques and pastoral experience both tell us that setting up classes and lecturing are not going to give us the educational results we seek. What will?

A primary educational challenge is to celebrate worship so well that more and more congregants hunger to know more about that which they experience. We have all seen congregations grow when the worship is vital and fruitful; we have also seen congregations diminish and sometimes even die out when worship is irrelevant, not God-centered, does not lead to mission. Over and above this, worship itself provides occasional opportunities to help people grasp more deeply the riches they celebrate. For example, when baptism is celebrated, even three or four lines about baptism plunging us into the death and resurrection mystery of Christ, repeated again and again, can go a long way to open people to who they are and what they are called to live. Preaching on these special occasions (other examples would be confirmations, marriages, funerals) present unique opportunities for challenging people to know more about their faith and what they celebrate.

Another way to educate congregants about worship is regularly to include short bulletin pieces on some worship element; this is especially important if a new element has been introduced. The real key to successful worship education is persistence and repetition. We must always remember that we are dealing with great mystery;

no wonder we do not "catch it" the first time around! Further, worship itself is a fairly recent discipline of study in theology (developed largely during the last of twenty centuries of church history). We have only scratched the surface; research, reflection, and new discoveries continue at a dizzying pace. Worship education challenges us to keep up with worship developments.

A further challenge of worship education is to have the tools at hand for adequate and responsible critique of our worship services. Too often worship is judged by feelings, by what the folks like or dislike, or by what is familiar and comfortable, by what binds us together more closely as a social community. None of these is an adequate measure of good worship — indeed, the only real measure is whether worship engages us in the mystery of Christ and his saving mission. We must always strive for worship services that remain ever faithful to the tradition of the church at the same time that they challenge the modern person to grow in his or her celebrating and living the gospel of Jesus Christ. We counter diminishing attendance and participation, boredom and hostility with worship that is so engaging as to be transforming.

Ultimately, the best worship education leading to worship renewal is that which becomes part of who we are and is so engaging that it helps us see the service beyond individual worship elements to something that is lived. In this way, worship comes alive — not simply because of the music or the preaching or the symbols or gestures, but because it is has burst its doors. This leads us to our fourth challenge.

THE FOURTH CHALLENGE:
WORSHIP BURSTING ITS DOORS

Although worship on Sunday is of primary importance, it is not enough simply to be there, as we said at the beginning of this chapter. Most worship services conclude with a *missio* — with a sending forth to live what we have celebrated. To encounter God and each other at worship equips us for mission. Worship by its very nature leads to a kind of spirituality, a certain way of living. This means that our way of living is liturgical (characterized by dying and rising) and worshipful (characterized by a life of praise and thankfulness for God's largesse expressed in sharing that with others who are the Body of Christ). The unique challenge of spirituality grounded in our worship lies between two poles — preparing well for worship and taking up our *missio* to share in our daily living what we have received from God.

If the hour or more spent at Sunday worship is all the time in a week we give God, we can pretty well assume that time will be boring. A good celebration of worship *demands* preparation — not only by worship planners and leaders, but by everyone who chooses to come. One preparation is the way we live — the challenge is to *live* the gospel so that we are "primed" to celebrate it. One practical pastoral suggestion is to help people express the paschal-mystery dying and rising in the rhythm of everyday living. Challenging people to enter more deeply into the rhythm of the paschal mystery helps mark our lives as liturgical and worshipful in profound ways.

Another preparation necessary for good celebration on Sunday is daily, quality personal prayer. As we surrender our personal time to spend time with God in prayer, we are also rehearsing the kind of surrender necessary for worship to be effective in bringing us to encounter God and be transformed by that encounter. Sometimes we might take time to be together with others for prayer during the week. Family prayer can be very powerful, but all too many families have lost any sense at all of the need to pray together. Many congregations offer a midweek worship service, but they usually are not as well-attended as the Sunday services. Bible study groups can be wonderful occasions for shared prayer. If we come to God in all of these different ways, they open us to the wonders of prayer and condition us to come to Sunday worship ready for prayer and hungry for deeper prayer.

We do not come to the Sunday service "cold"; we come ready because of the way we live. As we enter more deeply into spirituality grounded in worship as a way of living, then worship is not something we "go to" but instead becomes the *passion* of our lives — that which engages us with God, motivates us to right living, and gives us hope when our lives seem askew and distant from God. Then, let our passion lead to compassion! When this happens, worship has burst its doors.

Another challenge of worship bursting its doors (that is, living a worship spirituality) is that our lives witness to justice and reconciliation — right relations and healing and unity among all peoples. The reason for this is not based in philanthropy or even simply goodwill toward all. The reason that worship compels us to right relations and reconciliation rests in our identity, in our being the Body of Christ. Since we share this common identity (as daughters and sons of God) and a common mission (as disciples of Jesus to spread the Good News), it is inconceivable that we wish ill to another or are alienated from another. To wish ill toward another is to wish ill toward ourselves; to be alienated from another is to be alienated from ourselves, since we Christians all share the same identity as the Body of Christ. Right relationship with God means that we are in right relationship with each other.

This is a common theme that runs through the Old Testament prophetic literature. We cannot offer God right sacrifice if we are not in right relationship with each other. The "widow, orphan, and alien" are the symbols for this right relationship because the widow had no material means for support, the orphan had no family, and the alien had no homeland; it was the responsibility of the com-

munity to provide sustenance, family identity, and land that would
assure security (the Hebrew root for "salvation" originally meant
"possession of the land").

The *missio* of worship — being sent to live what we have celebrated — always empties us of ourselves, challenges us to take up
our daily cross of self-surrender, and spread the Good News as
Jesus did. The stumbling block for good celebration of worship
is that we will not remain the same when we prepare and celebrate well. We know this instinctively. This is why sometimes we
are tempted to gloss over the prophetic challenge of liturgy to be
transformed into ever more perfect members of the Body of Christ
and instead to settle for mere good feelings. We are "protecting
ourselves" from the challenge of self-surrender. But in so doing
we relinquish our greatest power — to change the world because
we have changed ourselves. This is what is at stake in celebrating
and living worship that has burst its doors.

Rather than being discouraging, these challenges are a constant reminder to us of what is at stake at worship: risen life in
God, in the Son, and by the dynamism of the Holy Spirit. Ultimately, ours are the same challenges as those faced in the past:
to open ourselves to God's work within us, to live the dying and
rising mystery of our baptismal promises, to recognize all as
brothers and sisters in the Body of Christ. Alone, meeting the
challenge is impossible. Jesus' promise that he is with us in all
things until the consummation of the world (see Matt. 28:20) is
what sustains us and carries all of us to that day of final glory. It is
no small thing to proclaim our identity as the Body of Christ. This
is who we are. This is how we live. The Christ within us empow-
ers us to say with great passion, "We are the Body of Christ who
has burst through any confining doors to be present to others as
God has chosen to be present to us." And to that, let the people
say "Amen!"

....

Reflecting Pause

Worship compels us as individuals and as a congregation to burst out the doors when . . .
Those to whom worship most compels us to reach out are . . .
We — as individuals and as a congregation — need to further our worship formation in these areas:
A spirituality of worship that can be lived both individually and communally looks like . . .

....

Worship in Action

Worship spirituality is far deeper and more complex than simply doing for others. A worship spirituality might be described as "worship in action" — which means that our whole lives become an act of worship. This means that everything we do ultimately goes to God's honor and glory, whether we are consciously aware of it or not. Worship spirituality is "putting on Christ" (Rom. 13:14), "wearing" Christ as our garment of salvation, never being separated from God. It means acting Godly in all things.

Worship spirituality suggests to us that Christian living is shaped primarily not by morality, fear of punishment, or specific religious practices, but by worship itself. Worship is the primary locus for discerning our stance before God and each other, and the two cannot be separated or be different from each other. Moral and virtuous living is the *fruit* of good worship; when separated from worship, morality by itself does not function very well to motivate us to wholeheartedly choose a gospel way of living. This is perhaps the most radical challenge of worship that transforms: an unprecedented deep entry into the very heart of the Christian mystery, which is Jesus' very life and ministry as a pattern for our daily living. This vision of worship in action offers us unprecedented opportunities for encountering our loving God in the other. The vision offers us unprecedented insight into who we are, why we are, and how we ought to be. We are good, charitable, joyful, forgiving, reconciling, moral, just, and so forth *because* we have been conformed to the very person of Jesus Christ at worship. Ultimately, living the gospel is God's saving work unfolding in us and through us.

This vision of worship spirituality is a shift from doing to being, from receiving to participating, from conformity to transformation. The shift in who we are is from being sinners (although we do remain that) to being together the holy Body of Christ. The shift in why we are is from keeping commandments that we have received (although we must do that) to participating in Christ's life and saving mission through our baptismal covenant of love and discipleship, which is grounded in our election as beloved sons and daughters of God. The shift in how we ought to be is from living this life in conformity to religious practices in order to receive happiness in the next life to realizing that our transformation during worship is already a share in the fullness of God's divine life.

This shift from morality to worship as the primary locus for our worship in action radically turns our lives upside down. Religion and worship can no longer be things "out there," things we "do" or "go to." Instead, religion (from its root meaning) is that which *binds us* in a unique relationship to our Trinitarian God, and that relationship defines for us a way of living. Liturgy is the ritual expression of that unique relationship to God — to the Father through the Son and in the Holy Spirit. Inescapably, what is at stake in the locus of our worship in action is not how we behave in this or that situation but who we are (which is really what determines our choices and behaviors). Our primary activity or expression of lived worship is our surrender to who we are (who God is making us to be). When we surrender to God's action, then our lives, too, are transformed. We live differently because we are different.

Let's face it: our everyday lives tend to be pretty messy. Fatigue, demands on our time, personality conflicts, distractions, ambitions, fears, illness, poverty, work, drugs, violence, war, displacement — all this and more can easily dissuade us from surrendering ourselves to God's transforming love. Worship, in contrast, is "home." Its familiar celebration patterns and consistent invitation into God's ways are like salve that helps us surrender. This worship surrender forms us into life surrender. Surrender during worship expresses our trust and faith in the God who loves and saves. It is that surrender that forms our willingness to surrender in our daily living to self-giving for the good of others — all others. Worship surrender leads to transformation of self. Then we cannot help but be moral, just, forgiving, and so on.

Worship in action must be a commitment on the part of every single congregant if the worship is to be vital and true. It is a commitment of one's spirit (spirituality) to surrender to this most sublime of God's actions within us. Only by surrendering to God's transforming action during worship can we think of living worship in our daily activities. So, "living worship" really has a double meaning. On the one hand, it is a spirituality that prepares us for fruitful worship; on the other hand, it is living the demands of the gospel in such a way that we witness to worship's hold on us. Worship in action is not pie-in-the-sky spirituality. It is a demanding one that prepares by our everyday living the kind of dying and rising that are essentially what we do during worship. So, all this is a bi-directional relationship: worship defines gospel living, and gospel living informs worship.

It takes great effort during worship (and patience with ourselves) to allay distractions, focus on God's presence to us in the community gathered, and let go of our desires, trusting that God will fill us. Even as challenging as full, conscious, and active participation during worship is, this is still not enough. Worship in action calls us also to participate fully, consciously, and actively in the world around us. It calls forth from us continual change in ourselves. At the same time, worship in action is so rewarding that it gives us a share in the life God offers — and gives it not only to us, but through us to others. Our everyday living is worship in action when we are turned toward the God in others with the same care, compassion, love, forgiveness, and desire for good that God through the risen Christ and in the Holy Spirit showers on each of us.

The notion of worship in action appears fraught with mystery and wonder — and it is! This is so because worship affords us the space to empty ourselves in praise and thanksgiving to the God who loves us into being, invites us to share in divine life, and trusts us enough to bring this same love and life to others. Perhaps even more mystery-laden than God's presence to us during worship and the offer of divine life to us is that this same God chooses us to be that same divine presence for others. How can we not embrace a spirituality that is worship in action? How can we not surrender our very selves to the good of others as both an expression of and a rehearsal of the dynamic that happens between God and us during worship?

....

Reflecting Pause

To us, "worship in action" means . . .
We experience worship taking hold of our daily living when
  we . . .

Our congregational spirituality looks like ... We wish it would look like ...

We have a sense that our daily lives inform our congregation's celebration of worship in these ways:

....

Worship and Doing Justice

Worship compels us to do justice not as something apart from it but as something integral to it, because just persons is what worship transforms us to be. And to the extent that worship is communal (for example, our Sunday services), then that solidarity with others reminds us again and again that we live in relationship with others. What matters to us affects others. What is happening with others affects us. It is not possible to reflect on worship's sending us forth to live worship spirituality, to continue Jesus' saving mission, to be God's presence in our world without reflecting on worship and doing justice.

FIRST, A (LONG) NOTE ON JUSTICE

Far too many of us think too quickly of "social justice" when the word "justice" comes up. Surely there is a time and place for everyone's active involvement in social justice issues, and sometimes there is a specific call to some people uniquely gifted to minister full-time in this important way. But let's face it. Not everyone is a Martin Luther King Jr. or a Mother Teresa. We must take care not to think that the relationship of worship and justice only applies occasionally to all of us when we are moved to write a letter to our government representatives or applies primarily to those engaged in social ministries. Justice has a broader venue: all of us are called to live justly.

To be sure, justice is social by its very nature. Both biblically and theologically, justice refers to right relationships; justice is the standard for living in community and establishing relationships among its members. One concern throughout the Bible but especially in the Old Testament is that all people have their basic needs fulfilled — among these would be land, food, clothing, and shelter. In this regard, it is telling to look at the proscriptions in Scripture for the jubilee year. (See Leviticus 25:1-55, where the basic requirements for the jubilee year are spelled out.) Every fiftieth year, land was returned to the original owners, wrongs were righted, and debts were forgiven. Every fiftieth year, the slate was wiped clean, so to speak, so that everyone had a chance to have what they needed in life, beholden to no one. Every fiftieth year, everyone could start over again.

This is one reason why so often in the Old Testament justice concerns the rights of the poor. The notion of justice, however, goes beyond this to include living rightly in all aspects of life. Further, justice not only involves right relationships within the human community, but our right relationship with God. Closely associated with this is the notion of "righteousness." We are considered just or righteous when we are in right relationship both with God and with each other.

One recurring theme — especially in the psalms and prophetic literature — is that one cannot worship (be in right relationship with God) unless one is in right relationship with members of the community (see, for example, Pss. 9, 72, 113, 140, 146; Mic. 6:8; Amos 8:4-6; Jer. 22:15-16; Isa. 58:6-7). One reason for this is that God is creator and sovereign of the world; everything that is comes from God. We offer God worship because God is creator and because God has called a people to be God's own. Worship is our response to all that God has done for us, our acknowledgment of God's greatness and of our being created by God. At the same time, worship demands of us a respect for God's creation and God's people. To put it another way, we cannot worship God in a vacuum; our relationship with God necessarily involves our relationship with each other because Creator and created are inseparable. This is one way that worship is related to justice.

Another way to get at this relationship is to reflect on a familiar Gospel parable, that of places at the table (Luke 14:7-14). Jesus is dining in the house of a leader of the Pharisees and notices "how the guests chose the places of honor" (v. 7). One approach to the parable is simply from a human perspective of social standing and saving one's face. It is embarrassing to take a place of honor and then be asked to move elsewhere; it is pleasing to sit at a lower place and then be asked to move to a place of honor. The parable might, however, be interpreted in a different way. The clue comes when, after telling the parable, Jesus instructs a host to "invite the poor, the crippled, the lame, and the blind" (v. 13). The point is not to invite guests who can repay the host in kind. Rather, Jesus admonishes us to invite those who cannot repay themselves; the host will be repaid by God "at the resurrection of the righteous" (v. 14). This special meal is called "messianic" when it includes those who have less than we have; the meal becomes the occasion to share equally in God's gifts of the land so that everyone might share in the abundance of God's blessings. By choosing a lower place at table, we align ourselves with the poor and needy; we acknowledge our relationship to God as creature to Creator. In a sense, this choice is a profound act of worship, for we witness by our action to a right relationship with God through our relationship with others. Further, being one with the poor means that we have firsthand knowledge of their plight and are better able to meet their needs, to serve them.

It is most telling that this chapter (fourteen) from Luke's Gospel concludes with Jesus making some rather harsh remarks about the cost of discipleship: "Whoever comes to me and does not hate father and mother, wife and children, brothers and sisters, yes, and even life itself, cannot be my disciple" (Luke 14:26). Jesus concludes with "So therefore, none of you can become my disciples if you do not give up all your possessions" (Luke 14:33). Giving up all possessions makes us all equally dependent upon God. It transposes our focus from our own needs and pleasures with its limited vision and restricted relationships to an enduring perspective derived from our most basic relationship to God — creature to Creator. The statement is not literally about the negatives of hating and giving up; it is about right perspective and right relationship. Everything we possess as humans pales in comparison to a single-hearted relationship with God and the gifts and blessings that brings. This is the basis for our human relationships with each other.

Now, let's be practical. This interpretation of the parable and of justice does not require us to give up asking our friends over for dinner! It does invite us to reflect on our own means — great or modest — and how much we share with others. This is not a matter of putting money in a "poor box" or donating to the local food pantry (though these surely are good things to do). The Scriptures remind us that justice entails *acting* on behalf of others so that right relationships are well-established. Moreover, as Thomas Aquinas reminds us, justice is a virtue or a *habit*. This means that serving others through meeting their needs — whether physical, spiritual, emotional, or psychological — is a *way of life* for us. Acting justly is not something we do once in a while when a special opportunity comes our way; it is a habitual way of relating. When we reach out to those near us, we establish good habits that help us see no real difference between doing for our immediate family, doing for our neighbor down the street, or doing for someone half a world away. All of our doing, then, will emulate God's pervasive care for all of God's creation.

Rather than the biblical notion of justice as right relationship, we generally tend toward the moral exposé of justice, especially following Thomas Aquinas. However, justice that lasts is more than "ethical" or "retributive" or "distributive" justice. These are theological terms and may be helpful, but they are not persuasive enough. The justice to which we are called by Scripture and worship is a pervading and invading justice. It is one that quickens at the very core of our being, making a difference in us and, therefore, in the world in which we live. Sometimes "the just" are thought to be those working directly with the poor, missionaries in Third World countries, the ones who are publicly trying to heal the ills of society. While all these kinds of endeavors are important, they can mislead us and entice us to forget that our very baptism sets us up in a relationship of common identity and that it is this shared being which is the impetus for doing justice, just as it is the impetus for doing worship. Who we are to one person, we are to all. We are all called to live justly and in right relationship. It is upon this that we will be judged (cf. Matt. 25).

We do not worship just to hear about how we should be in right relationship; we worship to celebrate the truth of that reality in our daily living. In other words, worshiping and being just are not two separate domains, but two dimensions of the one reality of being the Body of Christ living Jesus' saving mystery. If our lives are not marked by right relationships, how can we worship? These remarks dispel any dualism between the spiritual and the material, between God's world and our own. Justice calls us to live what we celebrate and celebrate what we live.

Justice, therefore, is the expression of who we are as baptized, committed Christians. It is not what we can leave to the "professional" missionaries or social workers, but it is constitutive of our relationship to Christ and each other in the Body of Christ. Ultimately, what counts is what *each of us* undertakes concerning right relationships. The world will not truly be whole until we look deeply inside ourselves and set right our gamut of relationships as much as we possibly can.

NEW SELVES LIVING JUSTLY

Being human means being born into the community of human-ity. Being Christian means being born into the dying and rising of Christ. Birth itself initiates lives turned toward justice because being born means to be in relationship with others. The wonder-ful gift of being called to worship is that we are continually called into God's divine presence, which transforms us into the presence of the risen Christ for others. Thus armed with God's perspective on creation and creature, we are better able to reach out to the "widow, orphan, and sojourner."

The relationship of worship and justice is reciprocal. Worship brings us the perspective we need to look upon all others as sisters and brothers in creation and in Christ. Being so related, choosing what is right and good for another is "natural." Doing justice — car-ing for the other, especially the other in need — opens us to the kind of self-surrender essential for worship to be transformative. Wor-ship transforms us for the sake of others; doing for others is "prac-tice" in the self-surrender that makes this transformation possible.

Living justly as transformed and new selves is a way of living (a worship spirituality) that focuses on the other rather than on the self. This is the "dying to self" demanded by commitment to the cross. It is the self-emptying kenosis that makes space for God's divine life to blossom within us. It may happen in the great things that the Martin Luther King Jrs. and Mother Teresas do; the world is a much better place for committed people like these. As wonderful as these actions on behalf of justice for others are, they are not enough. Worship and justice require that all of us — whatever our daily circumstances are — live as true disciples, having been sent to reach out and touch the leper, heal the sick, feed the hungry, teach the unlearned, set free those trapped by myriads of demons, and preach to the spiritually hungry. And, yes, it means raising those who are dead to new life.

....

Reflecting Pause

*We might participate in worship so that we are truly transformed
    more perfectly into the risen presence of Christ for others,
    living with God's perspective, in these ways:*
*With God's perspective, we view those around us — our fami-
    lies, our coworkers, our leisure companions, our worshiping
    community, the poor and disadvantaged of the world — in
    these ways:*
We respond to them in these ways:
*If justice means right relationships with God, self, and others, we
    cultivate this habit of right relationships in our daily living
    by . . .*
What needs to be changed in our lives to live this way is . . .
What gives us hope and courage in the face of just demands is . . .

....

Worship and Mission

Truly the Triune God gathers us for worship, and the Triune God
sends us forth. We do all in the name of the Trinity. God's action takes place (and, yes, it is primarily God's action), and we are
transformed into being ever more perfect members of the Body
of Christ; we are formed for mission. Only because of that transformation can we claim to be identified with Christ and continue
his saving mission. The essential connection between worship and
mission lies in the fact that worship continually plunges us into the
saving mystery of Christ, renews our commitment to live our identity as members of the Body of Christ, and pledges us to continue
Jesus' life and ministry in our own contemporary world. To be a

people living a worship spirituality is to be a missionary people. Two areas ripe for further comment emerge at this point. The first area concerns vocabulary and meanings. The second area brings us back to the relationship of worship and mission, which we will discuss in terms of the relationship of worship and life.

SOME KEY VOCABULARY

Each discipline — religious or secular — tends to have its own specialized vocabulary. Consider, for a moment, the new vocabulary coming out of the computer and Internet worlds: boot, byte, RAM, hard drive, flash drive, WiFi, text message, Web cam, blog, Web site, Facebook, Twitter, tweet — just to name a handful. Some of these terms have been around long enough that they have found their way into revised dictionaries. Philosophy surely has its own specialized vocabulary or words with specialized meanings, including "substance," "essence," "accidents," "process," and "Gestalt." Medical words, technical or engineering vocabulary, and literary terms are other good examples. So it should come as no surprise to us that theology in general and worship in particular have their own specialized vocabularies, too. Many worship terms have Hebrew or Greek etymologies (word origins) because our ancestors in the faith came from these two cultures. The brief comments here are not the last word on these terms by any means, but they may help to sort out what could be confusing concepts and meanings as we continue to reflect on the meaning of Christian worship.

Kingdom/Reign of God

In the Old Testament, the kingdom of God was equated with the kingdom of Israel; it was an actual land — the Promised Land given to the Hebrew slaves whom God had liberated from Egypt's power and domination. Originally God was the King of record; God's representatives on earth could be judges, prophets, or leaders such as Moses. Eventually the people of Israel asked for and received an earthly king; David is probably the best-known of Israel's kings. In the New Testament the sense of kingdom shifts dramatically and takes on a different meaning. There is a whole section of parables in Matthew's Gospel which begins with "The kingdom of God [or heaven] is like . . ." (a pearl of great price, for example). In these parables, Jesus (the Gospel writer) is clearly not speaking of a space or realm in the usual sense. Rather, the kingdom or reign of God has a double implication. On the one hand, we live here and now in God's reign, and we do so when we obey God's will (obey commandments; live gospel values), live up to our baptismal identity, and continue Jesus' saving mission. God's kingdom is present, therefore, whenever God's people acknowledge God's will and presence and respond with whole hearts.

But this reign of God that we presently experience is not all there is to what Jesus came to establish. So, on the other hand, God's kingdom always has a future aspect to it. God's kingdom is never complete, but is always "groaning" (cf. Rom. 8:22) toward its final fulfillment, when Christ will come in all his glory to end this world as we know it, rain down final judgment, and raise the faithful up in the general resurrection. God's kingdom, then, has an "eschatological" (see the next word, below) thrust. Christ's kingdom is not an earthly place but a way of living that derives from divine mercy and compassion, forgiveness and healing, love and care. Our mission is to help establish this reign of God.

Eschatology

Eschatology is made up of two Greek words meaning "the word on [or science of or study of] the end times [or last things]." Eschatology refers to the final fulfillment of God's reign, when Christ comes again at the end of time to bring judgment to the unfaithful and eternal life to the faithful. Jesus' own resurrection is a pledge of our share in his risen life and our own share in his risen glory. This raises the "tricky" part about eschatology. In one sense, eschatology refers to a future event when the end of time comes and final fulfillment of all people and things is reached. But we already share in Christ's risen life — we were initiated into it through baptism. In a real sense, then, we are already living in eschatological times. We are already sharing in Christ's risen life. We Christians are an eschatological community: we have one foot in risen life as we experience it through Christ's presence in his Spirit to us now; we have another foot reaching to the future time of fulfillment when salvation is definitively accomplished. Eschatology brings hope and direction to our mission.

Salvation

"Salvation" is probably one of the most frequently used words in the Christian vocabulary. Its Hebrew root word actually means "to be free from constrictions, from being bound, from narrow confines"; conversely, it means an enlarging, an opening up. God "saved" Israel when God brought the Chosen People from Egypt to the Promised Land — when God broke open the narrow confines of slavery and opened Israel to the new covenantal life with God to be lived in the Promised Land. From their earliest experience with God, Israel knew God as the One who offered salvation. Psalm 91 sings God's praises for rescuing us, sheltering us, guarding us, protecting us, delivering us, and satisfying us — in all this, God shows us divine "saving power." Jesus' name in Hebrew means "Savior," and through his life and ministry Jesus personified the in-breaking of God's desire for our freedom, God's desire to break the chains of whatever keeps us from being in relationship with God — a relationship so intimate that through baptism we are now called to be beloved daughters and sons.

This saving work is especially manifested in Jesus' healing, forgiving, compassionate, merciful ministry by which all those who came to have faith in him (opened themselves to his presence) were made whole. This wholeness was much more than a physical event; it was a process of coming to know Jesus, following him, and sharing in his life and ministry. Today we are engaged in this same process of salvation as we live as Jesus did with humility and openness and self-giving. Ultimately, salvation is about a share in the very life of God. Being saved is letting go of what confines us and opening ourselves to God's graciously abiding presence and life. Our mission is to continue Jesus' saving work.

Mission

We have all probably had the experience of seeing someone totally engrossed in some task or single-mindedly going somewhere and find ourselves uttering, "That person is on a mission!" To be on mission means to be engrossed in a task or journeying toward an end and allowing nothing to deter us from accomplishing what we set out to do. Jesus was sent by his Father to make known God's presence and will. Nothing — not even rejection and scoffing, suffering and death — deterred Jesus from why he became incarnate. He came to be God's saving, personal presence among us. In turn, as Jesus sent the disciples to go forth to announce the Good News to all, so are we also initiated into Jesus' saving mission — we become his followers, his disciples through baptism and our ongoing fidelity to the gospel. To the extent that we unite ourselves with Jesus, to that extent do we also unite ourselves with his saving mission. Like him, we cannot let anything at all deter us from doing what we are sent to do: making known God's loving presence, offering the hope of everlasting life, calling others to justice and peace. This is living the gospel. This is evangelization. Our mission is to be totally engrossed in gospel living and in making God's reign present by doing God's will.

Evangelization

From the Greek meaning "to announce good news," Christian evangelization is rooted in announcing the Good News (the gospel) Jesus came to preach and teach. Evangelization means cooperating with Jesus in making present God's reign. Just as with the prophet Jeremiah, who vowed not to announce God's word as God's prophet because of his persecution, but then could not hold in God's word because it became "like fire burning in [his] heart" (Jer. 20:9), so Jesus' gospel must become like fire in our hearts that we cannot hold in. Worship instills this heart-fire. Each of us, then, is a missionary because of our very relationship with the risen Christ in the Spirit. Each of us is sent to announce passionately by our words and deeds our relationship to the risen Christ, who makes present God's eternal life. Being evangelizers does not mean that we need to stand on a street corner and shout pious platitudes. It does not even necessarily mean that we go to some non-Christian people and try to convert them. It essentially means that we live the gospel publicly and with utter integrity. The best way to preach and spread the gospel is to live the gospel. This was the evangelizing way of the early Christians: they were known by their love. Our mission, ultimately, is to love as Jesus did.

WORSHIP AND LIFE AND MISSION

Formal, common worship is a "moment" during which we are immersed in Christ's risen presence and mystery, transformed into being able to live more perfectly his life and mission, and sent forth to live what we have celebrated. In a real sense, worship "rehearses" what Christian living is all about. It reminds us of who we are and how we are to live. Both worship and life are about Jesus and why he was sent by his Father: to announce salvation to all the world. Jesus' life is now our life. Jesus' mission is now our mission. Connecting worship and life and mission means that our celebrations — especially our gathering for the Sunday service — can no longer simply be "events" that we go to and leave as we please and that have little to do with our everyday living except perhaps some moral injunction we might glean from the readings or sermon. For too many people, worship is the only time of the week that they consciously turn their attention to God. Connecting worship, life, and mission means that we begin to see every moment of every day as turned to God, that God is truly the center of our lives, that God's will is our will, that Jesus' mission is our mission. This kind of a total turning to God has far more than moral implications. It means that our whole life becomes a kind of prayer (and, indeed, it means that we turn to God in prayer more than an hour or so a week on Sunday!). We begin to recognize that our very life is God's life, that all we have and do is gift from God, and that our most life-giving relationship is the one we have with God. Thus, worship steeps us in our very identity as the Body of Christ. It "remembers" for us who we are and what we are about. It opens us to the wider vistas of gospel living that touch everything we are and do. In short, it is a worship spirituality.

When we so identify worship and Christian living — when what we do in worship is what we do in daily living, that is, engaging ourselves in Christ's mystery of *kenosis* and exaltation — then the very expression of mission becomes the convergence of worship and life. We take up our mission to continue Jesus' life and ministry when our daily lives become "worship" replicating the surrender of each Sunday. Conversely, when our daily living is paschal, saving-mystery living — when it is "worship" — then our weekly worship comes alive not because of lively music or funny stories, or even because of gifted preaching, but because we are more attuned to God's transforming presence.

We are expressing here something far deeper than being sent from worship and doing good in our daily living. We are asserting that our Christian identity is so "at hand" for us that our essential mission is to live with the utter integrity of people whose being and doing, creedal expression and moral behavior, gospel values and kenotic self-giving choices meld into one act of worshipful living. Living this way — as Christ — is to *be* the mission. We announce by who we are and what we do — our words and actions — the Good News of salvation. This might seem an impossible challenge. How can I take up the mission of Jesus? To help us gain conviction, we might simply remember that we never celebrate worship alone (even when praying alone), but always as the Body of Christ. So it is with mission. We are never sent alone, but always as the Body of Christ, as church made visible. We are armed with the power of the Spirit, equipped with the wisdom of God's word, and supported by the love and gifts of the other members of the Body of Christ. In our very gathering for worship we already express our willing self-surrender to be larger than ourselves, to expand our horizons beyond our own limited vision, to have the mind of Christ (cf. 1 Cor. 2:16; Phil. 2:2, 5). In this act of self-surrender — giving ourselves over to being with others as the Body of Christ — we are living worship. We are proclaiming Christ's saving mission. *Ite!* Go! And when we do, we are being who God has called us to be.

....

Reflecting Pause

For us as a congregation to appropriate what it means to be sent,
worship needs to . . .
We feel sent to . . .
We most concretely experience having something to do with making God's reign present in the here and now when . . .
When we hear, "Go!" we want to . . . need to . . . hope to . . .

....

Conclusion

We have used many words in these chapters to talk about worship. And we have done so in two ways. The first two chapters largely focus on the "what" of worship; the last two chapters focus on the "who" of worship. In reality, these cannot be separated. Our reflections have, I hope, brought us to an understanding that the what and the who of worship are inseparable, and that in the very act of giving our Triune God praise and thanksgiving there is really no distinction between them. During Christian worship, we ourselves become that worship. That is, we ourselves become beings of praise and thanksgiving oriented to the God who created us, saves us, and loves us.

No single definition of worship can capture its fullness, its depth, its graces. Oh, yes, for academic and study purposes we might propose one or another definition of worship. Many scholars have done just that. But what our experience, data, and reflecting have brought us to understand is that worship is so much more than our words can capture. It is even so much more than what our experience can embrace. For this reason, as a kind of primer on worship understanding, these chapters have deliberately been left rather open-ended. There has been no real attempt to nail down a meaning of worship, but rather to open up meanings of worship. Unlike many books on worship, this book includes little history in its four chapters, little by way of church proscriptions about worship, little that might separate one denomination or communion from another. Instead, the intent is to be truly broad in scope, to initiate a conversation across denominational boundaries. Hopefully, by reading about ourselves and worship, we can be led to celebrate so much of what we have in common and put the differences into a larger perspective. This does not leave us without challenges; we will attend to those shortly. But it does invite us to a new way of thinking about worship that just might bring us to a deeper appreciation for how all of us Christians struggle with embracing a God who is so loving, so kind and merciful, so generous to us that, in the end, we are all simply left with praise and gratitude in our hearts.

Describing Christian Worship

If anything comes clear in all the words about worship in these four chapters, it is that words are not enough to capture the deeper, richer, mystery-laden meaning of worship. Nor even is a worship service, duly analyzed and evaluated, enough to give us a full picture of what worship is. Ultimately, what Christian worship is becomes a matter of reflecting on our lives; our priorities; and our relationships with God, self, and others. Obviously, this is not a simple process and cannot be accomplished in a short time. What Christian worship is comes clearer to us as a worship spirituality informs our life to the extent that every breath is oriented to worship. To understand worship, we must embrace gospel living!

But let's not duck the important issue of coming to some kind of formulaic description of Christian worship. The question of Chapter 1, "What, really, is worship?" is a question that needs to be addressed. Perhaps a very simple response with few words might be this: *Worship is surrendering ourselves before a loving and merciful God.* This brief statement includes offering (here rendered as "surrendering ourselves") and to whom we offer ourselves — "a loving and merciful God." Teased out of this statement would be an understanding that we are grateful to the Triune God, who has created us with such dignity, given us so much, and is aptly concerned with our health, wholeness, and well-being — that is, with our salvation. Our gratitude wells up as praise — the awe, respect, and adoration we offer God. And this God is, stunningly, not only a God who receives our worship, but who enables it and perfects it in Christ. The Triune God to whom we turn in worship is a God at work in us.

At the same time, any deep description of worship cannot omit encounter. So, we amend our brief statement from above: *Worship is surrendering ourselves before a loving and merciful God whom we encounter any time we open ourselves to the abiding Triune Presence.* Now our description is getting a bit longer, but we have added an important dimension to our understanding of worship: worship is not a uni-directional activity but is thoroughly bi-directional: we lift our hearts to God, and God reaches out through divine presence to be encountered by us. God does not remain in some far-off "place," but is present as we turn ourselves toward the divine Being who loves us so faithfully. In fact, God is even present when we turn ourselves away from the divine Being through infidelity! God is always willing to renew the divine covenant with us, even when we transgress (see, for example, Josh. 24:14-28 and Jer. 31:31-34).

No description of worship is adequate unless it mentions that worship must be lived. So, again we amend our description: *Worship is surrendering ourselves before a loving and merciful God whom we encounter any time we open ourselves to the abiding Triune Presence, a surrender and encounter that is played out in the relationships and circumstances of daily living.* Worship makes a difference in us (is transformative) and, therefore, makes a difference in how we live. This is especially true with respect to our relationships with others, relationships which reflect our relationship with God. Worship is not passive, not simply a response to the divine commandment; it is an active doing of what God does: commune with others. Further, if worship is to be lived, then it is lived in a particular time and context; in other words, all worship is inculturated. Worship is celebrated from within the context of how people are culturally united. If worship is to be meaningful, it will draw on the symbols, customs, habits, and ways of interacting particular to the people worshiping. One reality of Christian churches today is that very often our worship is multicultural — people of many different cultures come together to worship.

Worship always has an ethical import. So, again, we modify our description: *Worship is surrendering ourselves before a loving and merciful God whom we encounter any time we open ourselves to the abiding Triune Presence, a surrender and an encounter played out in relationships and circumstances of daily living that reflect our ethical choices and commitments, our concern and care for others.* But now our description is hardly short! It is becoming very similar to what some theorists call a "thick" description — that is, one that takes into account not only meanings but contexts. And now we are at a point where we can appreciate the depth and richness of worship. Our description can get longer and longer, but in the end we will never exhaust worship's wide range of attitudes, behaviors, elements, ramifications, and persons and their involvement. And this is, perhaps, where we need to be. Rather than "tack down" worship as something easily grasped, defined, and packaged in neat words that can too quickly be forgotten or become overly familiar and meaningless, we want to leave worship as open to deeper understandings and possibilities as we can.

The last word, then, needs to be mystery. Worship is a mystery that wells up in us awe, reverence, humility, gratitude, wonder, enjoyment, excitement, hunger, and numerous other human emotions and desires. Because, in the last analysis, any encounter with our Triune God leaves us breathless. But we do not die from lack of breath. We live even more fully because we are filled by the Spirit-Breath of God, who makes us one with each other and God.

The Challenges That a Fuller Understanding of the Nature of Worship Bring

Throughout these pages we have taken the position that Christian worship is not easy. It makes demands on us. Being cognizant of some of the challenges that a fuller understanding of the nature of worship brings can help us meet those challenges with courage and strength and conviction.

A first challenge is a reassessment of ourselves! So many things about us militate against the kind of personal surrender that Christian worship requires in order for worship to be fruitful. Some of the more at-hand personal challenges are distractions, busyness, lack of silence in our daily living, preoccupation with material things, and skewed priorities. Christian worship asks that we look at these things about ourselves and get our "house" in order. Some other personal challenges are more difficult to recognize and re-direct. Our values may well stray away from gospel values and the kind of life to which Jesus invites us. We all have a propensity for selfishness — to be preoccupied with ourselves — and worship calls us to experience ourselves as part of a community in which we are responsible not only for our own well-being but also for others'. Surprisingly enough, sometimes worship can even challenge us to evaluate our generosity. If we spend our time and resources exclusively on others, and we do not take care of ourselves and those given into our care, something is amiss. Worship challenges us to tend to the wholeness and well-being of ourselves — in other words, to our salvation.

A second challenge is the direction in which society seems to be leading us. In general, we no longer live in neighborhoods such as in times past, where people knew, supported, and trusted each other. In those times, neighborhoods often grew up around churches, so the shared religious values were obvious. For all kinds of complex reasons, including job opportunities, fiscal needs, wanderlust, and a desire for adventure on the part of our young folks, extended families and stable neighborhoods tend not to be the reality anymore. In addition, divorce and remarriage have radically changed the definition of the family unit. Children often grow up without knowing one or the other parent, without living with siblings, without the steady influence and traditions that grandparents, aunts and uncles, and cousins can bring. Too often, then, there is little reinforcement of the kinds of values and a gospel way of living that in past times were simply givens. Worship challenges us to be countercultural. To be faithful to worship spirituality and gospel values, we often must stand alone against cultural and social trends.

A third challenge arises from the congregation itself. "Worship wars" have been all too well documented. When a congregation cannot decide what its worship needs to look, sound, and be like, this is often an indication that not enough people have significant input into worship preparation, that there is little ownership by the congregants of the worship, and that there is little common agreement about what worship needs to be. In this scenario, worship challenges us to come to a common understanding and agreement about what the essentials of worship are. In this regard, it might be good to revisit the chart about the suggested differences between worship and liturgy that we considered in the first chapter. This continued reflection might also raise another important issue for a congregation: to assess whether worship is primarily personal, devotional prayer or whether worship is truly a communal expression of the congregation's commitment to aligning themselves with Christ and his saving mission. Perhaps a congregation needs to take a long, serious look at the similarities and differences of worship and liturgy. Perhaps this serious look would move them to a different way to assess the worship to which they attend each week: the reasons for it, its structural elements, its quality and fruits, the hopes and desires that are bound up in it.

Other challenges abound — for example, respecting and responding to the multicultural character of most of our communities and being inclusive with regard to race, gender, sexual orientation, socio-economic status, the mentally and physically challenged, and so forth. Sometimes church polity makes Christian worship difficult. At other times personal agendas of a subgroup within the congregation can cause havoc within a community. In all of this we must be brought back to worship as orienting ourselves to God and healthily toward each other, redirecting our insensibilities or narrow-mindedness to a more expansive inclusiveness, welcome, and charity.

For all of worship's wonder and challenges, in effect what is most helpful is to remember that worship is a privilege. Our Tri-une God — our Creator, Redeemer, Sanctifier — desires, heartily chooses to be present to us. Our God chooses to encounter us. Our God without fail chooses to love us. When we put this at the forefront of our reflection about Christian worship, then we can only be encouraged to surrender ourselves to the great good that is offered to us each time we take time out of time for worship. In the face of God, all the challenges are trivial indeed. In the face of the dignity God has conferred on us as creatures created in the Divine Image and called to be beloved daughters and sons, all the challenges are as nothing. To focus on coming to a deeper understanding of Christian worship and to commit ourselves to grow constantly in a worship spirituality is to embrace God's presence and life. And this is everything! It is a bit of heaven on earth. Then — and only then — can we understand how we can worship with gladness, with hearts filled to overflowing.

Index of Subjects

Adoration, 40, 54, 56, 78
Apostles' Creed, 41, 42, 89. *See also*
Creed(s)

Baptismal identity, 84-90, 95, 116,
118, 141
Blessing(s), 45, 47, 49, 54, 56, 71,
135, 136

Calvin Institute of Christian Worship, 31
Community: Christian, 20, 62, 84,
116, 117; eschatological, 142; human, 89, 134, 138; Israelite, 26;
liturgical, 27; living, 64; local,
22; social, 125; worshiping, 97,
121, 139
Compassion, 12, 38, 39, 56, 68, 73,
127, 132, 141, 143
Confession, 42-44, 50, 54, 56, 72,
76
Constitution on the Sacred Liturgy,
27, 99, 100, 101, 103, 104, 112
Contemporary: events, 25; music,
104; needs, 23; spaces, 66;
world, 139; worship, 27, 105
Conversion, 25, 28, 29, 44, 88, 120
Covenant, 58, 73, 87, 130, 151; Ark
of the, 72; baptismal, 88, 89;
life, 142; relationship, 61, 66
Creed(s): Apostles', 41, 42, 89;
baptismal, 41; Nicene, 41

Culture(s), 21, 23, 140, 152

Dialectic, 119, 120, 121
Dismissal, 47, 72, 115, 116. *See also*
Missio
East, significance of, 40, 85, 86
Education about worship, 123-25
Eschatological: context, 59; thrust,
141; times, 142
Eschatology, 141-42
Eucharist, 121. *See also* Lord's
Supper
Evangelization, 76, 78, 143, 144
Exaltation, 74, 93, 94, 96, 102, 113,
119, 145

Faith, 32, 41, 42, 45, 57, 63, 91, 116,
124, 131, 140, 143; profession of,
40-42, 89
Forgiveness, 12, 28, 41, 43, 50, 56,
68, 85, 90, 132, 141
Formation, 15, 18, 83, 129

God, Triune. *See* Triune God
God's will, 38, 45, 87, 120, 141,
144, 145
Gospel living, 41, 42, 47, 96, 126,
129, 131, 141, 143, 144, 145, 146,
150, 153, 154
Grace, 12, 32, 58, 60, 95, 111, 112,
118, 119, 149

Heavenly worship, 79-81
Holiness, 32, 44; God's, 58-64
Holy Spirit, 30, 62, 83, 88, 101, 113, 128, 130, 132

I AM, 77, 78
Incarnation, 49, 92, 93, 94, 118, 119
Intercession(s), 44-45, 71

Joy, 12, 16, 40, 56, 57, 67, 83, 95, 107, 119
Judgment, 30, 56, 62, 69, 117, 141; final, 116, 141
Justice, 17, 56, 68, 74, 127, 133-38, 139, 143

Kenosis, 93-96, 102, 109, 113, 119, 138, 145
Kingdom of God, 59, 88, 89, 140, 141

Lament, 54, 56, 70-73
Liturgical movement, 21, 99, 118
Liturgical year, 22, 29, 119
Liturgy. See Worship and/or liturgy
Lord's Supper, 25, 58, 62, 63, 71, 89. See also Eucharist

Minister, 20, 24, 85, 86, 106, 123, 133; ordained, 24, 46, 89
Missio, 126, 128
Mission, 47, 110, 112, 117, 118, 120, 121, 124, 126, 127, 139-46; Jesus' saving, 21, 28, 77, 91, 98, 116, 118, 120, 121, 125, 130, 133, 139, 141, 143, 145
Multimedia, 27, 36

Music, 23, 25, 27, 36, 103, 104, 123, 125, 145
Mystery, 35, 105, 117, 132, 150, 152; of Christ, 21, 33, 84, 87, 90-91, 94, 96, 100, 101-8, 111, 113, 118-30, 137, 139, 144, 145; paschal, 21, 22, 33, 86, 88, 90, 91, 92-96, 100, 101, 102, 113, 118-30; of salvation, 24, 93

Obedience, 92, 93, 94, 113, 120
Our Father (prayer), 37, 39, 43, 53

Participation, 62, 81, 91, 100, 104-6, 109, 110, 112, 113, 125; active, 104, 105, 106-8, 109, 111, 112, 113, 123, 132; conscious, 108-9, 111, 113; full, 109-12, 113
Paschal mystery. See Mystery: paschal
Pericope, 76, 77, 85
Petition, 20, 39, 40, 43, 44-45, 56
Praise: heavenly, 79-81; and Psalms, 65, 66
Prayer, 37-40; Eucharistic, 28; intercessory, 25, 27, 44, 45; liturgical, 29, 30
Preaching, 36, 71, 123, 124, 125, 146
Priesthood: high, of Jesus Christ, 81, 88, 89
Profession of faith, 40, 89
Psalms, 54, 55, 56, 57, 65, 105, 134; of ascendency, 65-69; of lament, 70-73; of thanksgiving, 73-75

Repetition, 40, 74, 124

Ritual(s), 20, 22, 24, 28, 45, 58, 86; and action, 26; and structure, 28

Sacrament, 25, 87, 94
Salvation, 16, 24, 25, 30, 41, 49, 62, 70, 71, 75, 90, 93, 97, 101, 119, 128, 129, 142-43, 145, 146, 151, 153
Second Vatican Council (Vatican Council II), 99
Service books, 23, 28
Sign, in sacrament, 22, 25
Silence, 47-50, 51, 65, 80, 105, 106, 107, 108, 153
Sin, 12, 16, 17, 35, 40, 42, 43, 44, 58, 84, 85, 86, 87, 94; forgiveness of, 41, 85, 88
Spirit, 31, 39, 76, 78, 79, 103, 131. *See also* Holy Spirit
Spirituality, 18, 117, 126, 127, 129, 130, 131, 132, 133, 138, 140, 145, 150, 154, 155
Sunday: as day of rest, 12, 48, 49, 102; why worship on, 42, 49, 102, 122
Surrender, 24, 42, 45, 66, 89, 97, 104, 108, 109, 110, 111, 112, 113, 126, 131, 133, 145; and baptism, 84, 88; as dying to self, 121, 122; to God/Christ, 13, 18, 64, 150, 151, 152, 153, 155; to God's presence, 73; to God's will, 38, 39, 120; of Jesus, 38, 39; to prayer,

21, 28; self-surrender, 128, 138, 146

Thanksgiving, 26, 33, 40, 54, 56, 66, 67, 69, 72, 73, 75, 81, 84, 89, 111, 132, 149; Great, 28, 71, 72; Psalms of, 73-75
Transformation, 70, 73, 97, 110, 111, 139; of ritual, 28, 113, 130, 131; and surrender, 120, 138
Trinity, 22, 30, 33, 139
Triune God, 12, 40, 41, 78, 139, 149, 150, 151, 152, 155

Vatican II, 99

West, significance of, 40, 85
Word: God's (Scripture), 22, 25, 53-58, 71, 72, 79, 84, 85, 103, 116, 144, 146; inspired, 58, 90; and sacrament, 94; and table, 33, 36
Worship and/or liturgy, 19-30; in action, 129-33; and doing justice, 133-38; elements of, 22, 36-50, 104, 125; and fixed texts, 20, 23, 25; heavenly, 79-81; intergenerational, 104; and life, 144-47; as lifestyle, 17; meaning of word, 20; and mission, 139, 144-47; prayerful, 27; and response, 69; style of, 12, 22, 27, 105, 106

Index of Biblical References

OLD TESTAMENT		20:26	60	1 Kings	
		21:6	61	19:11-12	65
Genesis		22:31	61		
1:1-2	48	23:2	61	**1 Chronicles**	
1:31	48	23:3	48	29:10-13	55
2:2	48	25:1-55	134		
2:3	48			**Tobit**	
2:24	28	**Numbers**		13:1-17	55
3:8	42	6:24-26	46, 54		
18:22-33	16	21:9	88	**Judith**	
				16:1-17	55
Exodus					
3:5	59	**Deuteronomy**		**Job**	
3:14	77	3:2-29	54	23:2-17	54
12:1-28	58	5:12-15	48	42:2-6	54
15:1-18	55	24:19-21	26		
15:20	55	32:1-3	54	**Psalms**	
15:20-21	72	32:1-43	55	8:5	35
15:21	55	33:2-29	54	9	134
19	65			13	70
20	65	**Joshua**		13:1a	71
20:8-11	48	24:14-28	151	13:1b	71
22:21-24	26			13:1-2	71
				13:2c	71
Leviticus		**1 Samuel**		13:3	71
11:44-45	59	2:1-10	55	13:4	71
17–26	59			13:5	71
18:2-5	61	**2 Samuel**		13:6	71
19:2	60	6:14	72	22:1	56
20:7	60	6:21	72	24	65

24:3a	65	97:2b	68	107:33-42	74
24:3-4	56	97:3	68	110:1	57
24:7a	65	97:6	68	111	74
24:7b	65	97:10	68	111:1-2	74
24:9ab	65	98	68	111:3b	74
28:1-5	74	98:1b	68	111:4b	74
28:3	74	98:2a	68	111:5a	74
28:6-9	74	98:3c	68	111:6b	74
30	74	98:4-9a	69	111:7	74
30:12b	74	98:9b	69	111:8b	74
31	71	98:9c	69	113	134
31:23a	71	99	69	116	74
31:24	71	99:5b	69	116:3c	74
51	54	99:7	69	116:10b	74
51:15	16	99:8b	69	116:17	74
62:12	57	99:9c	69	118	75
72	134	100	54, 66, 67, 68	118:1a	75
78:2	57	100:1b	67	118:1b	75
91	142	100:1-2	67	118:2b	75
92	74	100:3a	67	118:3b	75
92:1a	74	100:3b	67	118:4b	75
92:5	74	100:3c	67	118:19b	75
92:7b	74	100:4	68	118:21a	75
92:9	74	100:5a	68	118:22-23	57
92:12-15	74	100:5b	68	118:26	57
95	68	100:5c	68	118:28a	75
95:6	68	107	74	118:29a	75
95:7	68	107:1a	74	118:29b	75
95:7b	68	107:6b	74	136	75
95:8-9	68	107:8a	74	136:1a	75
96	68	107:13b	74	136:1b	75
96:3	68	107:19b-20	74	136:2a	75
96:7-8a	68	107:21b	74	136:2b	75
96:8b	68	107:22b	74	136:3a	75
96:10c	68	107:24	74	136:3b	75
96:13c	68	107:28b	74	136:4-25	75
97	68	107:29	57	136:26a	75

136:26b	75	**Hosea**		25:31-46	117	
138	74	6:6	17	26:29	59	
138:1a	74			26:39	38	
138:2b	74	**Amos**		26:42	39	
138:3	75	5:21-24	17	27:46	39	
138:6a	75	8:4-6	134	28:18-20	91	
138:7b	75			28:19	62, 86, 115	
140	134	**Micah**		28:20	128	
145:15	56	6:6-8	17			
146	134	6:8	134	**The Gospel according**		
147:9	56			**to Mark**		
150:4a	72			1:9	85	
		NEW TESTAMENT		1:10-11	85	
Ecclesiastes				1:12-15	29	
3:4b	72	**The Gospel according**		8:23	117	
		to Matthew		14:25	59	
Sirach		2:10-11	29	14:36	38, 39	
6:5-17	19	5:8	56	15:34	39, 56	
36:1-22	55	5:41	115	16:7	115	
		6:9-13	37, 53	16:15	115	
Isaiah		6:10	39, 45			
6:1	60	6:12	43	**Luke**		
6:3	54, 60, 79	6:26	56	1:46-55	53	
6:5	60	8:25-26	57	1:68-79	53	
6:8	60	9:9-10	117	2:10-11	29	
12:1-6	54, 55	9:12-13	42	2:29-32	53, 55	
26:1-21	55	10:7	115	4:1-13	93	
42:10-25	55	13:35	57	5:18-26	44	
58:6-7	134	16:24	95	9:23-24	29	
		16:27	57	9:51	115	
Jeremiah		18:20	24	9:51-53	29	
20:9	144	21:9	57	9:60	115	
22:15-16	134	21:28-31	93	10:27	54	
31:31-34	151	21:42	57	11:2-4	37, 53	
		22:43-44	57	12:7	35	
Daniel		23:39	57	12:22-31	35	
3:52-90	55	25	137	14	135	

14:7	135	11:41b-42	38	6:3-4	94
14:7-14	135	11:44c	115	6:4c	86
14:13	135	14:6	101	6:5-8	86
14:14	135	14:31	92	6:11	86
14:26	135	15:1-8	89	7:15-26	93
14:33	136	17:1-26	38	8:22	141
15	16	17:11	39	11:16b-24	89
22:19	21, 62, 94	18:5	77	12:1-2	54
22:20	58	18:5a	77	13:14	129
22:33	115	18:8a	77		
22:42	38, 117	18:14b	77	**The First Letter to the**	
22:44	38	18:19	77	**Corinthians**	
23:34	39	18:23	78	2:16	146
23:43	39	18:23b	78	11:17-34	62
23:46	39	18:24b	78	11:26	62
24:34	49	18:28	78	11:27	62
		18:29b	78	11:29	62
The Gospel according		18:40b	78	11:34	62
to John		18:42c	78	12	89, 91
1:1-5	84	19:26-27	39	12:14-27	27
1:10	84	19:30	39	15:54c	87
1:14	84	20:1	49	15:55	87
1:19-34	29	20:14-18	29		
3:1-8	87	20:17	115	**The Second Letter to**	
3:2b	88	20:21-22	49	**the Corinthians**	
3:3	88	20:27	120	5:21	12
3:4	88				
3:5-6	88	**The Acts of the**		**The Letter to the**	
3:14	88	**Apostles**		**Ephesians**	
4:4-42	76	2:1-38	29	4:12	27
4:9b	76	2:43-47	20	5:29-30	27
4:24	31, 32, 54, 76				
4:26a	76	**The Letter to the**		**The Letter to the**	
9:6	115, 117	**Romans**		**Philippians**	
11:28-44	38	6	21, 91	2:2	146
11:35	38	6:1-11	85	2:5	146
11:36	38	6:3a	83	2:5-11	55

2:6b	93	The Letter to the		7	80	
2:7b	93	Hebrews		7:12	80	
2:8	92	4:14–5:10	81, 89	7:14c	80	
2:8-9	92	7:1–8:13	81	8:1	51, 80	
2:9a	93			11:17-18	55	
		The First Letter of		12:10-12	55	
The Letter to the		John		15:3-4	55	
Colossians		4:20-21	43	16:5-7	55	
1:15-20	55			19	80	
3:16-17	54	The Revelation to		19:1b	80	
		John		19:1-8	55	
The First Letter of		4:8-11	55	19:3b	80	
Paul to Timothy		4:9	79	19:4c	80	
3:1-5	123	4:11	55, 79	19:6c	80	
3:1-7	81	5:9a	79	19:9b	80	
3:8-13	81	5:9b	79	22:17	80	
		5:9-14	55			
The Letter to Titus		5:12a	79			
1:5-9	123	5:14	79